C0-AXC-328

THY LIBERTY IN LAW

Walfred H. Peterson

BROADMAN PRESS
Nashville, Tennessee

51835

© Copyright 1978 • Broadman Press

All rights reserved.

4269–28

ISBN: 0–8054–6928–1

Dewey Decimal Classification: 261.7

Subject heading: RELIGIOUS FREEDOM//CHURCH AND STATE

Library of Congress Catalog Card Number: 78–59278

Printed in the United States of America

Preface

People who believe that religious faith is central to their lives ought to have a profound interest in religious liberty. People committed to spreading their faith must have a firm allegiance to that liberty. Yet there has been a lack of information on this subject, even among many church members. My purpose here is to begin remedying that lack. To do so, I have tried to show the large dimensions of religious freedom required by a Christian, to demonstrate that the demand for religious liberty is grounded in the Bible, and to outline the present law of religious freedom and church-state relations as developed by the United States Supreme Court. I do so as a partisan for religious liberty, though I hope that my bias has not corrupted my commitment to honest scholarship.

My debt to the many people who nourished my interest and expanded my knowledge in this subject is large. Here I especially wish to thank my family and my friends at Bethel College, at the Baptist Joint Committee on Public Affairs, and at Washington State University's political science department. Particularly, I owe much to a peerless teacher, C. Emanuel Carlson, and a wise, longtime comrade, Dalphy Fagerstrom.

To Marianne

Contents

51835

1
Religious Liberty Today: Some Starting Points

The Development of Religious Liberty

"Eternal vigilance is the price of liberty." This maxim is true both because liberty can be taken away by direct action and because the meaning of liberty, including religious liberty, is always changing. The change does not imply that yesterday's meaning was not adequate to yesterday's need. To the contrary, after Americans got rid of established churches in the eighteenth and nineteenth centuries (lagging Massachusetts finally disestablished churches in 1833), religious freedom for *most* people has been generally viewed as adequate in each succeeding generation.

Why does the meaning of religious liberty change if the society is satisfied with its definition? At least four factors give part of the answer.

First, while society in general may like its definition of religious freedom, not everyone or every group in society may like it. In this land of "freedom's ferment," [1] religious experiments have been many. Some of these experiments have challenged the accepted view of what is proper religious expression. To illustrate: Mormons believed that polygamy was proper— so proper that some of them practiced it. Yet, polygamy for any reason violated the law. Some of the stricter Amish groups still argue that they should not give their children formal education beyond the basic levels of reading, writing, and ciphering. Yet, state education laws require school attendance up to a set age. Such minorities—their roster is long—find it necessary to plead for a broadened definition of religious freedom compared to that required by more traditional religions. Some of these pleas have met with success, others have not.

Second, religious liberty's meaning changes as the technical conditions of society change. Freedom for an evangelist to preach the gospel once meant freedom to mount a stump and exhort those within earshot. With the development of loudspeaker systems, however, preachers could expand the range of earshot many times over. This irritated some people wanting peace and quiet. Inevitably, the United States Supreme Court had to decide what was the meaning of freedom for public address when using a loudspeaker. And the development of radio and television has forced the Federal Communications Commission to wrestle with issues of freedom of religion and the availability of broadcast channels and times.

Third, the meaning of freedom of religion must necessarily change as government powers and activities change. When the United States fought wars with volunteers, there was no legal problem for the pacifist who only objected to shouldering arms. He simply did not volunteer. But with the coming of the draft in the Civil War, a law of conscientious objection had to be developed, if the consciences of some were not to be offended. And when government did not regulate church-related hospitals and schools, those institutions' religious peculiarities did not produce legal tensions. But with the development of government regulation and subsidy, affected church-related agencies found that some of their previous ways of operating were questioned. Could they refuse to hire otherwise well-qualified persons because of their religious identification or its lack? Could they put religious symbols in their public rooms?

Unknown to many Americans, probably the most dramatic change in governmental power touching religious liberty was the growth of federal judicial power relative to that of the states. Up to the 1930s, it was good constitutional law to argue that a person's claim to religious freedom against any state government could be defended only by use of that state's constitution and its courts. That is, the First Amendment was aimed only at the federal government. In 1940, the United States Supreme Court handed down a precedent-breaking decision in *Cantwell* v. *Connecticut.*[2] It held that the word *liberty* in the Fourteenth Amendment, which expressly limited the states, included religious liberty. Therefore, the federal courts could decide cases on religious freedom that touched state actions. A whole new era of legal activity opened, for, in a general way, the federal courts were much more generous to claims of religious freedom than were state courts.

Fourth, the scope of religious freedom is affected by the attitudes of society in general. As these attitudes change, the definitions of religious freedom will almost certainly alter. Today, there is a demand for government monetary support for private religious schools so that both parents and children will be financially able to express their religious convictions by patronage of church-related schools. This demand is a product of changed attitudes respecting the scope of government, the role and value of the public schools, and the meaning of freedom itself. Once society looked upon freedom largely as freedom *from* government. Today, more people include in their idea of freedom the thought that for some purposes freedom requires government aid.

Thus, even though religious liberty has been generously defined over the years in American law, it remains an issue. Freedom's dimensions are always in flux. "Eternal vigilance is the price of liberty."

The Dimensions of Religious Liberty

Since most true believers assert that their religion is relevant to the whole person and to all of life, the dimensions of religious liberty must be large indeed. This point requires emphasis because the phrase, "freedom of worship," is used as a substitute for freedom of religion. It is no substitute.

Unfortunately, the phrase became much popularized

when President Roosevelt announced the "Four Freedoms" in his message to Congress in 1941. One of the four was "freedom of worship." Later that same year, the president and Prime Minister Churchill made the "Four Freedoms" part of the Atlantic Charter, an effort to rally anti-Nazi forces.[3] These freedoms received much press space during World War II. The popular artist, Norman Rockwell, painted a widely reprinted picture on this theme—a picture that was being sold in the form of a silver plaque thirty years later.[4] All this made the phrase commonplace.

The poverty of the phrase can be seen at once by analyzing the passage on religion in Article 124 in the Constitution of the Soviet Union. It reads, "Freedom of religious worship and freedom of anti-religious propaganda is recognized for all citizens." Clearly, the words are unfriendly to the scope of religious activity. It means *only* freedom of worship. Thus, a great deal of what can be done in more libertarian lands by way of religious activity cannot take place in the USSR. Religious education of the youth and wide use of religious publications, for example, are sharply limited there.

To understand the height, length, and breadth required for a really free religious expression, one must think of all that people think and do in the name of religion and remember that religion has both an individual and a group dimension. Thus, religious freedom must be freedom for the person acting alone and for groups of people acting jointly.

Let us develop two lists of activities required for a full measure of religious liberty.

A. The first list relates to the needs of individuals. They should be free to:

1. worship or not to worship;
2. choose their own creed and tenets;
3. join or not join a church;
4. change church membership without hindrance;
5. nurture the faith of children for whom they are responsible, controlling their education;

6. express their faith and convictions to others;
7. travel for religious contacts;
8. associate and assemble with others for corporate religious interests;
9. use property for religious purposes;
10. determine the causes and amounts of their religious contributions;
11. shape their life-styles to conform to conscience;
12. make moral judgments on public issues and express them.

If the list seems long, the reader should be warned that all its items have been the occasion for conflict somewhere in Western history.

B. The second list relates to the needs of the religious group—the church. It should be free to:

1. order its own worship services;
2. develop its own creeds and doctrines;
3. determine its own organizational structure, government, and membership rules;
4. set standards and qualifications for its clergy;
5. provide and control programs for leadership training;
6. provide education for its members and youth;
7. plan and carry out efforts at missionary outreach;
8. own and use properties related to its objectives;
9. raise money in lawful ways;
10. assert equal legal status with other religious and related groups;
11. formulate its own social and moral criticism of the society;
12. express its insights to the public and to other agencies in society.[5]

Clearly, the lists overlap and are mutually supportive. Clearly, they describe a liberty of broad dimensions. No mere "freedom of worship" or such restrictive phrase can begin to cover these requirements. Religion must treat all of life. Religious liberty must, therefore, reach life's most remote corners.

Three Levels of Religious Liberty

The two lists just presented must be recognized for what they are—an effort to spell out the details of religious liberty's meaning by a sympathetic advocate. The advocate began from a *theory* of religious freedom. The lists are demands or declarations. They are not necessarily *law*. Nor are they necessarily the *practice* of all of the American society or its official and unofficial agencies.

Discussions about liberty in general and religious liberty in particular often become confused because theory, law, and practice are not distinguished. To illustrate: some people argue on the basis of Thomas Jefferson's ringing words in the Declaration of Independence that we have the right to revolution. True, we do according to Jefferson's historic words. But they are only a declaration. They have no legal force. If a person began a revolution against the United States, the federal government would use force to curb it. The use of force would be unquestionably legal. Indeed, American statutory law— the Smith Act of 1940—says specifically that it is a crime even to advocate and teach the violent overthrow of government. Courts' opinions have clarified (or modified) that statute by saying that mere *abstract* advocacy or teaching of revolution was not covered when Congress passed the law. Abstract advocacy of anything is acceptable. Any law attempting to end it would violate the First Amendment's clauses on freedom of expression. But advocating or teaching *concrete* revolutionary action does violate the law, and a revolutionary who so teaches or so acts can go to jail.[6] Thus, a long-standing theory about the right of revolution put forward by the Declaration of Independence—the birth cry of the United States—has no standing in American law! It never had. Remember the Civil War? Remember the Whiskey Rebellion?

Let us move one step further. Even if the law defines a right clearly, the society may not let a person exercise that right freely. Economic pressures of various sorts or social pressures may inhibit a person from the exercise of the right. While courts say that a person can abstractly advocate or teach revolution, if a person tries to do so in some times or places, he or she might lose a job or might be obstracized by family and friends. Not only do theory and law differ, but law and practice also differ.

Careful discussion of freedom then must distinguish between these three levels of rights: theory, law, and practice. Otherwise, the discussion will create confusion. One participant will be talking on the theoretical level; the second will be hearing what is said but may be thinking on the legal or practical level. A famous religious liberty case decided by the federal Supreme Court will illustrate how these levels can be confused. It is *Cantwell* v. *Connecticut,* handed down in 1940.

Cantwell, a Jehovah's Witness, stopped passersby on the street, asked them to listen to his phonograph record, and offered to sell them literature. His record attacked organized religious groups and especially the Roman Catholic Church in very offensive terms, calling them, among other names, "instruments of Satan." On one occasion the two people he stopped became angry. One threatened him with physical violence. Cantwell picked up his phonograph and literature and started to walk off.

Then a policeman arrested Cantwell. He was later charged with breach of the peace and with raising money for his religious cause without first getting a certificate from the local public welfare council allowing him to do so.

Cantwell's lawyer argued that the law of freedom of religion protected him from both charges. He needed no certificate to sell his literature or ask for contributions for his religious group. He could not be charged with breach of the peace because his freely expressed religious views caused anger in those who at first said they were willing to listen.

In the Connecticut courts, Cantwell lost his case. Given the history of Jehovah's Witnesses, we can be sure that Cantwell had something of a theory about religious liberty. He would witness regardless of the law, for he was divinely obligated to do so. Human authority could not control him on such a matter.[7] But, alas for Cantwell, Connecticut law did not accept this theory. Further, citizens of Connecticut threatened him with physical violence when he gave his witness. Theory was contradicted by both law and practice.

But Cantwell's lawyer thought he could win this case by going to the United States Supreme Court. He made application, the Court accepted the case, reviewed it, and gave a verdict in favor of Cantwell. The verdict had two distinct elements, each very crucial to the total American law of religious freedom.

First, the Supreme Court had to justify its considering the case at all. Cantwell's lawyer had appealed by claiming that his client's religious liberty had been violated. Doesn't such a claim relate to the First Amendment's free exercise of religion clause? Doesn't that clause limit only the federal government? How can it relate to a state matter? As noted above, the Supreme Court for the first time in a clear way said that the protection given religious liberty by the First Amendment was made applicable to the several states by its inclusion in the Fourteenth Amendment's phrase, "Nor shall any *state* deprive any person of life, *liberty,* or property, without due process of law" (italics added). For matters of religious freedom, states were then and there limited in the same way as the federal government by the Bill of Rights.

Second, the verdict said that this constitutional protection shielded Cantwell from both charges against him. The certification requirement, said the high court, gave too much power to a local official to determine what was a religion, and the policeman had no cause for arresting Cantwell for breach of the peace when other people got aroused over Cantwell's expression of religious opinions. The implication was that the short-tempered passerby should have been arrested if breach of the peace were at issue.

Thus, because of the United States Supreme Court, Cantwell's theory of his religious freedom was found to be closer to the American law of free expression than Connecticut judges would have it. But as many Jehovah's Witnesses would later find, a Supreme Court decision does not protect a person in practice from angry people, including policemen, in the short run.

If the Witnesses are right about the great day of the millennium, then theory, law, and practice will be harmonized in heaven. There the highest of courts and the chosen few will put things all together! But here on earth, the three levels of liberty are not necessarily harmonized. Indeed, for people like Cantwell, it seems almost to take a miracle to make them so.

What can we learn from Cantwell's travails besides the fact that freedom has several dimensions? Importantly, even in a very free society the struggles over freedom go on and on and on. As long as people have different ideas about their freedoms, some will find the law and practice of the society inadequate. We can expect them to complain and/or resist in some way. Isn't that the hallmark of a free society? Freedom does not produce uniformity.

The Plan for What Follows

The chapters that follow will be organized around the three levels of freedom just outlined. First, a theory of religious liberty will be presented. One theory among many, it is designed to fit the mind-set of Christians, finding its basis in the Bible. Second, the relationship between theories of liberty and the law of liberty will be discussed. Third, in three chapters the American law of religious liberty—mostly found in United States Supreme Court decisions—will be laid out and assessed. Separate chapters on the law will take up church-state relations and tie these relations to the issues of liberty. No discussion will be needed to cover American practices of religious freedom, for the reader will see how people have lived out their freedom in the many court cases we explore.

Hopefully, all this will not just educate. It is meant to make the reader a firm champion of religious liberty in every proper way.

Notes

[1] The phrase is from Alice F. Tyler's *Freedom's Ferment* (New York: Harper Torchbooks, 1962).

[2] Cantwell v. Connecticut, 310 U.S. 296 (1940). An earlier case had anticipated this development, but since in it the appellant lost, its value as a precedent was a bit unclear: Hamilton v. Regents of the University of California, 293 U.S. 245, (1934).

[3] Richard B. Morris, *Encyclopedia of American History* (New York: Harper and Brothers, 1953), p. 365.

[4] *Saturday Evening Post*, November, 1974, pp. 64–65.

[5] C. Emanuel Carlson, "The Meaning of Religious Liberty" (Washington, D.C.: The Baptist Joint Committee on Public Affairs, undated).

[6] Dennis v. United States, 341 U.S. 494 (1951) and Yates v. United States, 354 U.S. 298 (1957).

[7] *The Truth that Leads to Eternal Life* (Brooklyn, New York: Watch Tower Bible and Tract Society, 1968), pp. 157–163.

2
The Biblical
Basis of Religious Liberty

The Need for this Discussion

A solid biblical basis for religious liberty exists. This point needs a vigorous defense and a special emphasis for several reasons.

First, in the history of Christendom many good and faithful believers imagined the Bible taught religious repression rather than religious freedom. Alas, over the centuries they and their churches persecuted or caused governments to persecute both non-Christians and other Christians solely because of divergent beliefs. In the sixteenth and seventeenth centuries this persecution came to a depressing climax in brutal executions, imprisonments, and banishments of Catholics by Protestants, Protestants by Catholics, Protestants by Protestants, and unbelievers by Christians. True faith, it seemed, had to be protected and promoted by cruel violence.

Those who commanded and applauded the persecution thought they did so on the basis of the Scriptures. They were wrong, and their beliefs hindered the development of the idea that the Bible promotes free belief, expression, and action. Not until 1965 did the Roman Catholic Church change positions on this matter, and within some Protestant groups today, respecting their own internal affairs, there is little concern for, or even hostility to, freedom of religious thought and action. Thus, the biblical case for freedom must be made and emphasized.

Second, many American Christians support freedom solely

on grounds of a natural law argument borrowing from a thinker like Thomas Jefferson, who found the basis for freedom in those self-evident truths he described so eloquently in the Declaration of Independence. The borrowing from Jefferson was to be expected in American experience, for this tied the argument to one of the most respected champions of freedom. This authority could help win debates. Further, in the history of political thought, it is but one ideological step from Jefferson back to England's John Locke and but a few more back to the Catholic Church's great natural law theorist, Thomas Aquinas. Thus, American Catholics and many Protestants, who shared much Thomist thought, inherited a strong natural law tradition which they believed or merely assumed was compatible with their biblical starting points. Since the compatability between a biblical perspective and a natural law perspective is debatable,[1] it will help freedom's cause for many if the claim to be free can be founded in Holy Writ.

Third, the biblical basis needs development and stress because too many Americans—Christians and non-Christians alike—make their claim for freedom only on the basis of what appears in the Bill of Rights. "The First Amendment to the Constitution gives us religious liberty," it is said. Obviously, this is wrong. Words written in documents have meaning only as people—governors and the masses alike—act on them and define them. Liberty lives in hearts and minds not on paper, however much it helps to have the printed word to refer to in case of disputes. Remember, there was the phrase "equal protection of the laws" when blacks were denied equality in dozens of ways. Thus, the grand and useful phrases of the Bill of Rights can be hollow in practice unless people give meaning to those phrases on the basis of their deepest beliefs. For Christians this means that the Scriptures must give content to our legal freedoms if Christians are to be their champions.

This raises the final and the obvious point about the need for a biblical defense for freedom. Christians commonly say in their official or unofficial creeds that the Bible is the infallible guide to all of life. If so, where will freedom rank in Christian values if it is not found in the Scriptures? To be sure, no one consciously wants to warp the Bible to make it fit what he happens to prefer. Hopefully, the argument made here is not based on my preference but on the letter and spirit of the biblical message. If so, freedom in a paradoxical way becomes a requirement the Christian is not free to ignore.

The Biblical Assumption of Religious Liberty

Bluntly put, no explicit defense of religious freedom that could be called a whole theory is presented in the Bible. Rather, references there that might be fitted into a whole theory are scattered, brief, and often more implied than direct. These references are commonly a part of a narrative about how people acted. Action, not theory, is the context for most biblical expressions about religious freedom. Further, the actors are not involved in struggles for religious freedom as such. Typically, they are simply responding to a divine call requiring that they proclaim their message.

In the Old Testament, the prophets denounced their government's policies and actions as if freedom were simply assumed. Their mission required it, and that was that. Once a priest tried to forbid the free expression of Amos, and that prophet responded with a doom upon the priest that still sends a shudder through the reader (Amos 7:10–17). When threatened with death for his prophecy, Jeremiah is recorded as simply saying, "The Lord sent me to prophesy against this house" (Jer. 26:12). Isaiah walked three years naked and barefoot as a "sign and wonder upon Egypt and Ethiopia" (Isa. 20:3). Words and dramatic demonstrations were the taken-for-granted tools of the prophetic trade.

The same simple assumption appears in the New Testament. When Peter and John were told not to preach in the name of Jesus, they replied, "We ought to obey God rather than men" (Acts 5:29). And elsewhere in the book of Acts, the early Christians are said to have gone about giving their witness in spite of private and public threats. Thus, Old and New Testaments are of one piece in this matter. A person with a divine message must declare it in spite of what people and authorities say to the contrary. Freedom is assumed, but nowhere is the assumption systematically laid out and defended.

Biblical Themes Appropriate to Religious Liberty

There are, however, several interwined themes related to the biblical view of God and mankind that fit or are appropriate to a theory of religious freedom. Three will be treated under this heading, and a fourth, because of its special importance, will be treated alone.

First, throughout the Scriptures it is asserted and assumed that human authority of all sorts—state, family, church, etc.—is not the final authority for the individual and for the group. God may use human authority, but God is always above that authority judging it, as the references to the prophets and the book of Acts just cited imply. Human authority, then, is not necessarily and finally valid.

True, "the powers that be are ordained of God" (Rom. 13:1), but those powers are subject to God's order. They are given power for human "good" (Rom. 13:4). They are to operate within a limited sphere as is seen in Jesus' words, "Render therefore unto Caesar the things that are Caesar's; and unto God the things that are God's" (Matt. 22:21).[2] When a government acts evilly or outside its sphere, interfering with the true religious duties of people, it is denounced in devastating terms. Further, the true believer is not to obey it at that point. (See the book of Revelation, especially chapter 13.)

A second element of biblical perspective harmonious with a theory of religious liberty has been referred to already. It needs expansion here. God specifically orders persons and groups to act. That is, the Bible promotes a kind of individualism and a kind of social pluralism.[3] The lonely prophet is told to go to the king's court and excoriate sin there. The early

Christians, individually and collectively, were told, "Go ye, therefore, and teach all nations" (Matt. 28:19).

This means that in the Scriptures there is no necessary "chain of command" that runs from God through the state, the church, or other human institution to the individual or lesser group. Rather, God often chooses to ignore institutional hierarchies, giving orders directly to a person or group. Unless it is assumed, contrary to much experience, that human institutions will always be attuned to God's purposes, this disregard for the "chain of command" will force the person or the group called to some special task to disregard contrary orders and restrictive rules of other human agencies. The youth feeling a mission to become a minister may well have to disregard his family's requests or even parental orders.

Perhaps the words may sound startling, but the Bible can easily be read as radically individualistic and/or pluralistic in style on this matter. This reading would be wrong, but its possibility must be acknowledged. The single person or the group can be set out against all other human authority. A simple diagram may help clarify this.

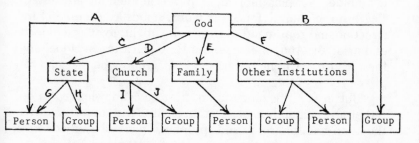

The arrows at A, B, C, D, E, and F represent God's directives for action. Arrow C, going to the state, may be passed on by the state to the person or group in some legal way, represented by arrows G and H. So too with the arrow D, I, and J, etc. But always there is the possibility of arrows A and B. That is, institutions may be disregarded. And in the Scrip-

51835

tures and in Christian history, the arrows at A and B may put people at odds with the state or at loggerheads with their church, their family, and so on.

If it is objected that this view is a dangerous idea to social unity or to the health of the state or the family, a sound rejoinder is in order. In the biblical ordering of values, the individual is central in the here and now compared to institutions. Salvation in the New Testament is directed toward the person—each person alone. When people talk of the "salvation of the state" or "the salvation of the church," they are using *salvation* in a special and rather poetic sense—not in the most important biblical sense. Further, the individual becomes central to the carrying out of some divine purpose if chosen for that purpose. Think of Martin Luther: "Here *I* stand; *I* can do no otherwise."

But a warning is needed. Finally, the Bible is not radically individualistic when the individual is considered or radically pluralistic when the religious group is considered. While people or groups alone may do their thing, there are biblical controls on this individualism and pluralism that *should* work to prevent its being radical in some ultimately negative sense. Scripture is a guide by which individual and group actions are tested. The historic church, for all its faults, stands as a source of instruction and reprimand to those who might go off some deep end or other. And, of course, the Holy Spirit leads. Hopefully, these controls will help the person or group who takes a prophetic role not to err.

But in fact this observation must be acknowledged to be rather abstract and theoretical. Look at Christian history. Ten thousand splinter groups and "prophets" have all claimed some special mission that others not only did not share but also actively opposed. And all claimed being guided by the Spirit, the Bible, and by the "true" traditions of the church. Thus, while controls exist on the divisiveness of the individualism and pluralism we have described, they are in actuality not always effective.

Importantly, it must be conceded that the person or group

ordered by God to do this or that need not use that order as a justification for claiming religious liberty. Instead, they can quietly act and suffer the consequences—becoming martyrs, perhaps. But likely as not, people put in such a hard place will plead for religious liberty in their suffering. Like Roger Williams, banished from Massachusetts in the winter of 1635–36, they will demand "soul liberty" where conscience can find a haven—unless, of course, like those who drove Williams from Massachusetts, they organize a colony where their consciences alone determine what is proper and legal.

A third biblical theme appropriate to religious liberty is inherent in the way the Christian message is spread—"by the foolishness of preaching" (1 Cor. 1:21). Persuasion, oral or written, is the human tool of the Christian witness. Whatever the Spirit of God does to bring conversion, words of people are vital to the process. True, the silent witness of some saint may persuade, but only after someone has explained what motivates the saint's life. True, pantomime and drama may also be effective, but this only amplifies the point. Communicative persuasion is the tool.

This need for persuasion requires that the means of persuasion be available. Translated into terms of American law, the need finds its means in the thrust of the First Amendment of the Federal Constitution. "Congress shall make no law . . . prohibiting the free exercise [of religion] . . . ; or abridging the freedom of speech, or of the press; or of the right of the people peaceably to assemble."

Again, the need for persuasion does not absolutely require the freedoms just described. Freedom of religion being denied, the present-day Christians in the USSR continue to give their forbidden witness. The Soviet expatriate, Alexander Solzhenitsyn, has given us the powerful picture of Alyoshka, the Russian Baptist, in a prison camp in *One Day in the Life of Ivan Denisovich*. But the need for persuasion strongly urges that freedom be allowed. After all, Alyoshka's lot is miserable, and most people would wish him better. The blood of the martyrs can be the seed of the church, yet that fact scarcely argues that in a decent society blood should flow. But, admittedly, the Scriptures tell us that God's work will get done in spite of human perversities, including repressive laws.

The Crucial Fourth Theme

Ordered together, the three themes just described can give something of a biblically based theory of religious liberty. In thumbnail form it goes: God who finally controls all people and institutions makes demands upon them of various sorts. Some of these demands include the living of and the declaration of the Christian life. Where some people or institutions interfere with God's demands upon other people or groups, the interference cannot be used as an excuse for disobedience to God.

Nowhere, however, does the Bible go on to say that legal and social liberty are mandated by God. It makes its demands on the person or group; it does not flatly state that the society or the government must organize itself somehow to promote religious freedom. Thus, it was necessary to admit that the Bible could be read as if it required martyrdom rather than legal and social freedom.

Logic, not biblical passages, may point to freedom from what has been said, but it is logic that forces the demand. This logic appears in the book of Acts in the crisp words of the Jewish leader, Gamaliel. He, a Pharisee and doctor of the laws, told the Jewish high priest and others to permit early Christians to continue their witness as they felt required. His words bear quotation.

Ye men of Israel, take heed to yourselves what ye intend to do as touching these men. For before these days rose up Theudas, boasting himself to be somebody; to whom a number of men, about four hundred, joined themselves: who was slain; and all, as many as obeyed him, were scattered, and brought to nought. After this man rose up Judas of Galilee in the days of the taxing, and drew away much people after him: he also perished; and all, even as many as obeyed him, were dispersed. And now I say unto you, refrain from these men, and let them alone: for if this counsel or this work be of men, it will come to nought: But if it be of God, ye cannot overthrow it; lest haply ye be found even to fight against God (Acts 5:35–39).

If this account helps ensure that a case for religious freedom can be grounded in the Bible, it still falls short of guaranteeing a biblical theory of liberty that many people would call minimal today. Why? Because, it could be read as a plea for a limited freedom for a certain kind of religion.

Gamaliel was a devout Jew. He may have recognized that early Christians were something of a sect within Judaism. They always started debates from the Old Testament. They claimed to have recognized the long, hoped-for Messiah when others had not. Perhaps Gamaliel had toleration for only certain ranges of religious expression. Would he have been so liberal if he had been confronting pagans proclaiming the deity of some golden calf?

The question is terribly important, for it must be regretfully conceded again that on the basis of the Bible, Christians—Orthodox, Catholic, and Protestant—have supported persecution of false religion and atheism. That is, many have argued that the Bible supports freedom for only "true" religion.

For some fifteen centuries the Roman Catholic Church more or less officially took the position that there could be the restriction of freedom for false belief or for disbelief. Truth alone merited freedom, and the truth was known to the Roman Church. Truth could not be a matter of mere private opinion.

Further, this traditional Catholic view claimed that a well-ordered state had an obligation to promote the expression of the truth and suppress or, at least, retard the expression of the false. Resting on an argument that went back to Augustine and on the nineteenth-century encyclicals of Pope Leo XIII, Cardinal A. Ottaviani could argue as late as 1953 that:

The Pope appeals to justice and reason, because it is contrary to justice to accord the same rights to good and evil, to truth and to error.

Reason rebels against the idea that, to satisfy the demands of a tiny minority, the rights, the faith, the conscience of almost an entire nation should be injured; and that this nation should be betrayed by permitting those whose aim is to set snares in the way of its faith to introduce into it division, with all the consequences of religious strife.[4]

While the cardinal's argument rests on "justice and reason" rather than any rehearsal of biblical passages, the Roman Catholic Church, and some Protestant churches as well, long assumed such a position was rationally defensible from the Bible. Most Protestant groups shifted, or were forced to shift, away from this position by the brute facts of continuous religious splinterings in the seventeenth, eighteenth, and nineteenth centuries. In the process of this shift, some like Roger Williams, developed biblical arguments to support their new position.

Happily for freedom's cause, the official Roman Catholic position was dramatically changed in 1965 by the Second Vatican Council. Then it declared that the demand for freedom, including religious freedom, was "greatly in accord with truth and justice." [5] In its "Declaration on Religious Freedom," the Catholic hierarchy made an effort to justify their new stance. They did so by an appeal to human dignity as found in the Scriptures. Here are the key paragraphs:

The declaration of this Vatican Council on the right of man to religious freedom has its foundation in the dignity of the person, whose exigencies have come to be more fully known to human reason through centuries of experience. What is more, *this doctrine of freedom has roots in divine revelation,* and for this reason Christians are bound to respect it all the more conscientiously. Revelation does not indeed affirm in so many words the right of man to immunity from external coercion in matters religious. It does, however, disclose the dignity of the human person in its full dimensions. It gives evidence of the respect which Christ showed toward the freedom with which man is to fulfill his duty of belief in the Word of God and it gives us lessons in the spirit which disciples of such a Master ought to adopt and continually follow. Thus further light is cast upon the general principles upon which the doctrine of this declaration on religious freedom is based. In particular, religious freedom in society is entirely consonant with the freedom of the act of Christian faith.

It is one of the major tenets of Catholic doctrine that man's response to God in faith must be free: no one therefore is to be forced to embrace the Christian faith against his own will. *This doctrine is contained in the Word of God* and it was constantly proclaimed by the Fathers of the Church. The act of faith is of its very nature a free act. Man, redeemed by Christ the Saviour and through Christ Jesus called to be God's adopted son, cannot give his adherence to God revealing Himself unless, under the drawing of the Father, he offers to God the reasonable and free submission of faith. It is therefore completely in accord with the nature of faith that in matters religious every manner of coercion on the part of men should be excluded. In the consequence, the principle of religious freedom makes no small contribution to the creation of an environment in which men can without hindrance be invited to the Christian faith, embrace it of their own free will, and profess it effectively in their whole manner of life.[6]

This concern for the dignity of each person becomes the fourth element of the biblical structure of religious liberty. Each saint or sinner is a sacred entity, enormously valuable in God's sight. The value is reflected in the biblical thrust, repeated from Genesis to Revelation, that each has the power of choice. Each can voluntarily respond to God's love and call. Even at the level of rejecting God's purposes, each person may choose for or against his own good. None is to be or can be tricked or bribed or compelled into choosing the good. People simply are not wired that way. Such a determinist wiring does not harmonize with the nature of God or man. Thus, coercion respecting belief is improper.

While not a poem that has appealed to many makers of Sunday morning sermons, "Invictus" by William E. Henley has a Christian dimension to it in spite of its tone. "I am the master of my fate; I am the captain of my soul."

The poem adds, of course, that at life's end the "scroll" may be charged with "punishments," and, admittedly, the Bible warns against wrong choices in awesome terms that some people would claim were equivalent to physical coercion. *But the biblical warning of punishment for wrong doing and belief is in a paradoxical way a most powerful testimony to its affirmation of freedom and the dignity that goes with it.*

The person is given freedom of choice in spite of the fact that God, concerned with that person's well-being, asserts that wrong choices are frightfully serious. That is; *my choices really count! Therefore, I count!* Here is the ground of dignity. Were all wrongful choices always automatically ignored and/or forgiven, all choices would be trivial. Then, I would be trivial. God's threat of judgment is the final proof that each person matters and that each person is a potentially free being.

Freedom and Faith

The four elements of a theory just described—a God above human institutions, giving mandatory missions to people and groups, to spread a message by persuasion, to persons of such infinite dignity that they ought not be coerced in life's greatest choices—are not indeed a whole theory of religious liberty. Such a theory would have to detail the nature of God, mankind, and the purpose of human institutions in much greater measure than was done here. But these elements of a theory point to the conclusion that there is indeed a whole theory of this sort logically inherent in biblical teachings. Further, these biblical themes make it impossible to argue for coercion respecting belief and its expression.

Unfortunately, it has had to be admitted that Christians and some of their churches for far too long did not recognize that this theory was found in the Scriptures. They chose to believe that true religion could be advanced if people were kept in ignorance of alternatives, if they were made church members by law, if the government certified a given religion as true and the only religion recognized at law, if that religion were the only religion taught in schools, if punishment or deprivations were used to persuade the wavering, etc.

Alas for good intentions promoted by wrong means! The reliance on these varied techniques of ensuring true belief by human means was always a fatal admission that those who used them did not believe that God was sovereign and that his work could be done by the means set out in the Scriptures—that is, by persuasion enlightened and aided by his Spirit. In short, those who did not or do not rely on freedom to produce true belief lack faith in the means of doing God's work characteristic of Jesus' patient and quiet way of teaching. They would use some form of human force to see that what they call God's work gets done.

Clearly, the way Jesus called his disciples and the way he taught are in harmony with the idea that faith in God's power requires freedom. Imagine his answer to someone who argued that religious belief and regulations should be protected or promoted by force of law. Would the answer not sound like this? They who promote belief by the sword will see their beliefs perish by the sword. What would Jesus say to someone who made sabbath observance legally mandatory? Would the answer not sound like this? Except a man keep the sabbath in his heart, he keeps it not at all. Or perhaps, he who keeps the sabbath for fear of a fine is like the Pharisees. And to try another example with a modern dimension—Would Jesus argue that an atheist ought not be free to broadcast on radio? Such an argument would seem out of keeping with the faith that made him resist the temptations to political power found in the account of his experience in the wilderness. Jesus spoke freely against the establishments of his day. I assume he would want the same right for others. "Do unto others" was his fundamental social rule.

Clearly, freedom requires a faith in the capacity of God's Spirit using his people to persuade, "Not by might, nor by power, but by my spirit, said the Lord of hosts" (Zech. 4:6).

Notes

[1] For a discussion of Protestant thought on this subject, see René de Visme Williamson, *Independence and Involvement: A Christian Reorientation in Political Science* (Baton Rouge, Louisiana: State University Press, 1964), pp. 152–160.

[2] With these famous words Jesus answered a trick question. Therefore an argument that the words should not be used in relation to a theory of freedom might be made. But the cryptic words fit so well with the rest of biblical teaching that they summarize it all. The fact that they are a clever response to a trap does not detract from their usefulness.

[3] By social pluralism is meant the organization of the larger society into many subgroups which have significant power and functions of their own.

[4] Cited in Giovanni Miegge, *Religious Liberty* (New York: Association Press, 1957), p. 23.

[5] "Declaration on Religious Freedom" (Washington, D.C.: National Catholic Welfare Conference, undated), p. 2.

[6] Ibid., pp. 8–9 (italics added).

3
Religious Liberty: From Theory to Law

A Warning

The theory of liberty, the law of liberty, and the practice of liberty will differ—so said chapter 1. There is a biblical basis for religious liberty—so said chapter 2. This chapter will take up some of the issues that arise when theory and law are jointly considered, giving an explanation for some of their differences. It begins with a warning to anyone wanting to make a direct connection between Christian thought and American law. The warning, implied in chapter 1, needs development.

The American law of religious liberty is not and cannot be based on any single theory of liberty—biblical or otherwise. Why? Ultimately because the United States is a very pluralistic and free land. This has meant and still means that Americans, both aware and unaware of it, live by many different religions or philosophies or world views—among them Protestant, Catholic, Jewish, Orthodox, agnostic, atheist, Buddhist, Muslim, and pragmatist. A complete list of American "isms" would be tediously long. These diverse world views give different bases for freedom if they support freedom at all. Further, even those people who claim to live their lives around one of the world views just listed—Protestant Christian, for example—differ deeply on what that outlook means and how it should affect the society's law and practice. Contrast an average Episcopalian with an average Quaker on the matter of justifying war. And just as sharp a contrast can be found within a single Christian denomination whose members say the same creed each Sunday.

In light of this wide diversity, American law cannot rest on a single coherent theory of freedom. If it did in a serious way, it would offend too many of us. Our diversity coupled with our belief in democracy requires that this people must be united on other grounds than religion or ideology. In the forceful words of Justice Jackson in a Supreme Court case which struck down as unconstitutional a state requirement that school children must salute and say the pledge of allegiance to the flag, "If there is any fixed star in our constitutional constellation, it is that no official, high or petty, can prescribe what shall be orthodox in politics, nationalism, religion, or other matters of opinion or force citizens to confess by word or act their faith therein." [1]

The justice's idea was not new in 1943 when he wrote those words. At important points in our history we have recognized it. *American democracy had and has no single ideological starting point, no single basic orthodoxy.* Paradoxically, its lack of an ideological starting point is its only possible starting point. No ideology is its ideology.

Of course, many people, past and present, disagree with this idea. They feel it necessary to ground our national unity in some single, basic belief pattern which, if not held by all, still influences most. Otherwise, they say, there can be no unity.

Not so! Clearly, we have been united in spite of our diversity for two hundred years. How can it be explained? Let us take a giant leap backward some three and a quarter centuries and listen to the earnest plea for allowing diversity of belief from that fervid Christian, the Reverend Roger Williams. Recall that he had been driven out of a "united " Massachusetts in the cold December of 1635 because he believed that Massachusetts' orthodoxy on the matter of church-state relations was wrong—contrary to the Scriptures. He founded Rhode Island squarely on the notion that religious unity was *not* essential to the secular (the word means nothing bad) and general welfare. He later wrote a sort of parable explaining his position.

There goes many a ship to sea, with many hundred souls in one ship, whose weal and woe is common, and is a true picture of a commonwealth, or a human combination or society. It hath fallen out sometimes, that both papists and protestants, Jews and Turks, may be embarked in one ship; upon which supposal I affirm, that all the liberty of conscience, that ever I pleaded for, turns upon these two hinges—that none of the papists, protestants, Jews, or Turks, be forced to come to the ships's prayers or worship, nor compelled from their own particular prayers or worship, if they practice any. I further add, that I never denied, that notwithstanding this liberty, the commander of this ship ought to command the ship's course, yea, and also command that justice, peace and sobriety, be kept and practiced, both among the seamen and all the passengers. If any of the seamen refuse to perform their services, or passengers to pay their freight; if any refuse to help, in person or purse, towards the common charges or defence; if any refuse to obey the common laws and orders of the ship, concerning their common peace of preservation; if any shall mutiny and rise up against their commanders and officers; if any should preach or write that there ought to be no commanders or officers, because all are equal in Christ, therefore no masters nor officers, no laws nor orders, nor corrections nor punishments;—I say, I never denied, but in such cases, whatever is pretended, the commander or commanders may judge, resist, compel and punish such transgressors, according to their deserts and merits.[2]

Of course, Williams was a far-out radical when he wrote his "ship letter." But his basic idea caught on in ever-widening circles and slowly became influential in shaping American law. The Deists like Jefferson grasped at Williams' idea because they feared and opposed the influence of organized religion in American life. The religious evangelicals like Methodists and Baptists grasped the idea because they feared and opposed the religious establishments of the Colonial and Revolutionary eras.[3]

By the time of the Constitutional Convention in Philadelphia, the federal charter of government could be drafted without reference to God or Christianity or any other ideological litany. What then was its basis for national unity? The secular well-being of the society as set out in the Preamble: "We the People of the United States, in Order to form a more perfect Union, establish Justice, insure domestic Tranquility, provide for the common defence, promote the general Welfare, and secure the Blessings of Liberty to ourselves and our Posterity, do ordain and establish this Constitution for the United States of America."

And at Article VI the founders said, "No religious Test shall be required as a qualification to any Office or public Trust."

While this article was opposed by many who would have required at least a sworn belief in God as a qualification for office, and while others complained of the omission of religious references in the entire Constitution, the document was ratified by the required votes. Further, the Bill of Rights added to the secular thrust of the Constitution by requiring that Congress could pass no law "respecting an establishment of religion."

Indeed, the idea of a sharp line between the sacred and secular for the federal government had so much acceptance by 1797 that a Federalist President, John Adams, could negotiate and a Federalist Senate could ratify a treaty with Tripoli which read: "As the government of the United States is not, in any sense, founded on the Christian religion; as it has in itself no character of enmity against the laws, religion or tranquility of Musselman; and as the said States never have entered into any way or act of hostility against any Mohametan nation, it is declared by the parties that no pretext arising from religious opinion shall ever produce an interruption of harmony existing between the two countries." [4]

And these Federalists felt more sympathetic toward Christianity and the churches than the Jeffersonian leadership which followed them into power in 1801. [5]

To be sure, the legal divorce between sacred and secular was not welcomed by all. Some state constitutions had and still have passages referring to God and to agreement on Christian principles. Indeed, not until 1961 could a person who would not take an oath affirming the existence of God hold public office in Maryland. In that year the Supreme Court struck down this requirement as a forbidden "establishment of religion." [6] And to this day some people propose a "Christian Amendment" to the Constitution. One version would have asserted that the United States "recognizes the authority of Jesus Christ," but such proposals have never made it out of committee in House or Senate.[7]

These observations mean this in respect to the law of religious liberty: When a person demands liberty from the government on the basis of his or her religious belief, that person is appealing to the law of a Constitution that serves all sorts of people, not to a Constitution logically derived from the teachings of that person's religion. Conflict may well result. To illustrate: a Quaker's plea to be exempt from military service for religious reasons must be made with reference to the meaning of the First Amendment and/or the draft laws passed by Congress. Neither the First Amendment nor the draft law was written to spell out the implications of "true Quakerism." Even where Congress spelled out the provision for the conscientious objector, the Congress did so without pretending to apply the logic of Quaker belief to American law. Inevitably, many Quakers who become conscientious objectors feel that the law which benefits them on this matter is at best only barely adequate to their needs. After all, it is a small part of a law that helps make it possible for the American government to wage war the whole world round, and many—not all—Quakers oppose that awesome possibility.

The Legal Starting Point: The Constitution and Constitutionalism

American theories of religious freedom, all of them, have one legal starting point when they are put into practice—the two religion clauses of the First Amendment to the federal Constitution. The relationship of the First Amendment to the law of the fifty states will be discussed later. The clauses' words are few—just sixteen. "Congress shall make no law respecting an establishment of religion, or prohibiting the free exercise thereof." Nowhere does the Constitution define these terms. They were not borrowed from well-developed British law on the subject. Since in 1791 when this amendment was ratified and today when we continue to use it, people differ on the legal meaning of "religion" and "establishment" and "free exercise," we must recognize that our constitutional starting point for freedom of religion is general or ambiguous or vague.

Of course, other clauses of the Bill of Rights and other articles of the Constitution give something of a context for the sixteen words. The First Amendment also says that there is to be no "abridging of freedom of speech, or of the press; or the right of the people peaceably to assemble." The Fifth Amendment protects "property" from being taken without "due process of law." And Article VI gives us the "no religious Test" for office clause. Other of the Constitution's descriptions of the powers, procedures, and limits on American governments are indirectly relevant to the religion clauses. Yet, taking all together, we are still left without anything approaching a clear meaning of the law of religious freedom or of the establishment of religion.

Why is there so little in our Constitution respecting those vital aspects of our nation's life? Why sixteen words on such broad matters? Only a part of the answer, important as it is, can be found in the fact that the founding fathers thought that matters touching religion were overwhelmingly the concern of the several states. Another part of the answer concerns both what a good constitution is and how it is made.

A good constitution is brief and general or ambiguous or vague on most—not all—major matters because it is a charter intended to last into the unforeseen future. As such, it cannot spell out in detail what the government should do on most things or even how a government should do what it does. The greater the detail, the less likely the constitution will endure. Tomorrow's special circumstances and novel problems cannot be prudently controlled by specific rules laid down today. Only a general guidance can be given if tomorrow is to take care of itself.

In American experience, some states have unhappily put much detail and specificity in their constitutions. A common result is that these constitutions are knowingly ignored or violated, directly or indirectly, by otherwise law-abiding officials. Why? Because they find that the amending process is too difficult or impossible or slow for the pressing needs of good government. A widespread illustration is found in the ludicrous maneuvers of many legislatures to get around fixed time limits—often ninety days every other year—set for their sessions. At least one legislature literally covered the clocks in House and Senate chambers on the fifty-ninth minute of the last legal day of meeting. Then it continued that last legal day for weeks, ignoring clock and calendar time. So much for a nineteenth-century constitution that contained details inappropriate to twentieth-century needs.

Also, a good constitution is likely to be ambiguous because it must be made by the art of political compromise. At least in a pluralistic and democratic society like ours there simply is not complete or substantial agreement on many issues. If the constitution-makers themselves or as agents of those who elected them reflect our pluralism, they must use ambiguous words to have any hope of finishing the draft of a constitution and having it ratified. If they insist on precise definitions or very narrow terms, they will be certain to generate opposition. To illustrate from American history, a Deist like Jefferson could accept the free exercise clause because he hoped it would help provide freedom *from* religion. A Methodist evangelist could accept the same clause because he hoped it would help provide freedom *for* religion. Using the unclear words, "free exercise," satisfied both people and their groups. Had the phrase "freedom from (or for) religion" been used, it might have been more clear, but it would certainly have caused friction. The founding fathers and the first Congress were trying to set in motion a new government. They could not afford much friction of their own creation.

Or take another illustration. The antiestablishment clause could be supported by both those who wanted no government support of any and all religions and those who might happily accept support for all religions without preference being given for any one of them. Both views could be found easily in 1791.[8] This is to say that both the Constitutional Convention and the first Congress that proposed the Bill of Rights were not assemblies too much different from political conventions and congresses today. Their membership had to grope and struggle for agreement. They could not start from some single well-refined theory of liberty or of government organization and spell it out in logically coherent and consistent terms. None of the participants was happy with their work. They all felt they had given away too much on many matters of importance. They knew full well that they had often resorted to glittering generalities.[9]

Does this mean the Constitution and the First Amendment are a sort of meaningless fraud? Not at all! Most Americans in 1791 wanted some sort of freedom of religion. They had moved beyond the notion that uniformity of religion was possible or, for some, desirable. Thus, there was enough agreement to call for "free exercise." Within that agreement, they could face future conflicts over exactly what that meant in terms of, let us say, the taxation of church property in Washington, D.C. And there was agreement that at least the national government should not create an established religion. Within that agreement, they could face the future conflicts over what that meant concerning the military chaplaincy. The words of the Constitution did create something of an agreed upon arena and some rules concerning how political combat in it should take place. Two hundred years under one constitution—a rare achievement—have shown that the words were well chosen.

To use the jargon of lawyers and political scientists, the men of Philadelphia and the first Congress applied the idea of constitutionalism to the twin concerns of religious liberty and church-state relations. That is, they laid it down in their few words that the federal government was limited in powers and in procedures respecting these matters. For the federal government, religion was to be either a private matter or a matter for the several states to control. That was and is a crucial agreement, even if its exact meaning was not spelled out.[10] Could one realistically ask that Massachusetts Congregationalists, Virginia Deists, and Pennsylvania Quakers agree on much more? Perhaps today one could, but in 1787 and 1791 when the memory of their British traditions and experiences was still fresh, one could not.

What does this imply for our overall discussion? An important thing indeed! All Americans whose religious beliefs require that they demand freedom under law have only one starting point. They can turn to the sixteen words precisely because those words are not precise. A Quaker opposing war on religious grounds can use them to oppose the draft. An Amish family opposing compulsory school attendance for their teenage children can turn to them to begin its case. A Baptist cadet forced to attend worship at the Naval Academy can turn to them to object to compulsory religion. An atheist opposed to prayers in public schools can turn to them to assert that opposition.

Clearly, if our government is to "let freedom ring," we must use those general and ambiguous words which will encourage people to pull their own bell cords of liberty. And Quakers and Amish and Baptists and atheists have found rich meaning and effective law in those sixteen words. The authors wrote well if freedom was their theme.

Who Defines the Starting Point?

From what has just been said, it seems that, paraphasing Alexander Pope, "For constitutions' terms let fools contest./ Interpreters of terms will rule the rest."

Perhaps an exaggeration, the point, however, has much

validity. Those who interpret the words of any constitution have important, even decisive, power.

Who interprets the terms of the First Amendment? Many people do. Some are government officials, others are not.

When legislators enact laws which affect the exercise of religion and the operation of religious groups, they interpret the words of the twin religion clauses. When chief executives sign such legislation into law or veto it, they and their advisors also interpret the terms. Very importantly, when administrators apply those laws to specific people or groups, they also interpret. Sometimes administrators, who believe that a law is unconstitutional, will alter the legislative intent as much as possible by the way they administer the law in an effort to make the law constitutional. And when judges hear cases claiming that this or that law or administrative action violates a clause in the Constitution, they too must interpret what the clause means. These comments apply to both state and federal officials as both are sworn to uphold the federal constitution.

A moment's thought will indicate that the official interpreters do not always act as self-starters. Often they are ignited into action because some person or interest group demands that a law be passed or that it be vetoed or that it not be administered in a way which they find hurtful or even that it be declared unconstitutional. This means that purely private people help interpret the terms of the Constitution. Usually, they do not come to government officials asking humbly for this or that interpretation. They come armed with the legal briefs of expert lawyers insisting that their interpretation of this or that constitutional phrase is the only proper interpretation.

For example, in the footnotes of this book, the name Leo Pfeffer is repeated many times. He is probably the most well-known expert in the law of the religious clauses of the First Amendment. His books are available in any good library. He has appeared before federal and state legislative committees, administrative officials, and courts regularly for some thirty years as a First Amendment expert. He, often as the attorney for the American Jewish Congress, presents a sophisticated and well-argued legal theory about the meaning of the religion clauses. People listen to his arguments because he can predict rather accurately what the Supreme Court will or will not accept by way of government action touching religion. I once wrote to him concerning a potential church-state issue in Seattle, Washington. From far-off New York came his swift reply which volunteered his services if the issue ever came to court. The career of this scholarly and opinionated lawyer shows that even one person can help point the society to new definitions of its constitutional terms.[11]

But isn't the Supreme Court the final interpreter of the Constitution? The answer is a firm *yes and no*. Yes, for those matters which can reach the courts and which the Supreme Court chooses to hear. No, for those matters that cannot be framed as a judicial dispute to the court's satisfaction. Certainly, the Supreme Court is the most authoritative interpreter of the Constitution where it can and will claim power to act, but it is far from the only interpreter of it. The case of *Walz* v. *Tax Commission* will illustrate this and several other points just made.[12]

In May, 1967 Frederick Walz bought a small bit of land in New York City. The tax commission routinely assessed the value at $100 and levied a property tax of $5.24 against Walz. Walz objected, but not over the amounts involved. Apparently he had bought the land for the sole purpose of challenging the constitutionality of the property tax exemption given by New York to churches. By being assessed the property tax, Walz acquired an interest in the New York property tax law that the courts might recognize. Without such an indentifiable interest no court would have listened to his claim.

What was the claim? Walz argued that churches benefited from the total governmental services of the state of New York, yet they paid no property tax. To him this meant that when he paid his property tax, he was indirectly making a contribution to religious bodies. This, he thought, not only violated his free exercise of religion by forcing him to aid churches but it also amounted to an establishment of religion. Being a lawyer, Walz knew that both the freedom of religion and the antiestablishment of religion guaranteed by the First Amendment against federal actions were made applicable to the states by the Fourteenth Amendment.

Since Walz knew constitutional law, he should have known that the case would be hard to win. Why? Because such tax exemption of churches had been a part of American history since the Revolution. It was written into both the New York Constitution and New York statutes. Also it was a part of the law of the other forty-nine states and of federal law for the District of Columbia. This meant that state and federal legislators had always assumed that church tax exemption did not create an establishment of religion or violate its free exercise when they passed or amended or reviewed tax laws. Governors and presidents had signed such laws, regarding them as constitutionally sound. Also in similar past cases some state courts had said that claims like those of Walz were not well grounded in the First Amendment's words. Hundreds of people had already, in effect, decided against Waltz's plea.

Why then did Walz take this costly route in an effort to overturn church tax exemptions? Beside the fact that he must have been a natural-born crusader, there were two reasons: First, Walz probably thought that his First Amendment claim had absolutely no chance of being accepted by the regularly elected branches of New York state government. After all, state legislators and a state governor are not at all likely to commit political suicide by offending all churches and church people who would not approve such a shift in tax law. Only the judges, somewhat insulated from political change, might support him. Second, the United States Supreme Court, since it first said it had power to hear cases against states relative to the free exercise and the establishment of religion, had developed a reputation for interpreting the antiestablishment clause in a rather strict way. Recall that twice in the 1960s, it had held that the very old and widespread practice of having religious devotions in public schools was unconstitutional under the establishment clause. Thus, to go to court and to the Supreme Court became Walz's best and last resort.

Walz, of course, had to start at the bottom. His claim was rejected by the New York Tax Commission, then by the appellate division of the New York Supreme Court and after that by the New York Court of Appeals, that state's highest court. These losses should have dampened most of the optimism the litigant had. Why? Because the New York courts said they were applying the law of the First Amendment as the United States Supreme Court had interpreted it. But on Walz went anyway.

To the surprise of most students of the First Amendment, the United States Supreme Court granted Walz a full hearing. The surprise resulted from something that only a persistent person would ignore. In both 1962 and 1965 the Supreme Court had refused without explanation to hear two very similar cases from Rhode Island and Maryland. Notice, this refusal shows that the Supreme Court can pick and choose among the thousands of cases brought before it annually.

When the highest court of the land indicated it would listen to Walz's arguments, many other people became active. To his aid came the American Civil Liberties Union with a whole battery of skilled lawyers. They submitted an amicus curiae (friend of the court) brief on his behalf which the court accepted. So too did the Society of Separationists, headed by the well-known atheist, Madalyn Murray O'Hare, who earlier had been a successful litigant against prayers in public schools and later was an unsuccessful litigant respecting whether astronauts could pray over their government radios from outer space. These groups came forward for several possible reasons. One is this: Though a group is sure the case will be lost, it will still want the case to be argued as well as possible from its perspective. Even in a loss, the court might write an opinion that is *relatively* satisfactory to some loser.

The state of New York, of course, continued to oppose Walz's argument. But now the state found it had friends of legal convenience also. Thirty-five states and Puerto Rico filed amicus curiae briefs supporting its position. And eight religious agencies—Protestant, Catholic, and Jewish—also filed briefs, as did a secular agency, Americans United for Separation of Church and State. These briefs, while not necessarily agreeing with New York's constitutional argument, all asked that the Supreme Court approve New York's tax exemption for, at least, houses of worship.

So, over forty agencies and many more lawyers were finally involved in this case. All were trying to settle the meaning of the First Amendment in a way they thought was proper. The many arguments made did not all agree—even those on the same side. Clearly, the First Amendment's clauses mean different things to different people, including expert lawyers. They are bones of contention around which opponents circle in anger.

May 4, 1970 arrived, the day of the decision. It had been two years and eleven months since Walz had started his case in New York, not a really long period for such efforts. Chief Justice Warren Burger delivered the majority opinion of the court. Justices Brennan and Harlan concurred with the chief justice—that is, they agreed with his decision but not with all his reasoning. Each wrote separate opinions. Only Justice Douglas dissented. Walz lost eight to one. Why?

The chief justice's opinion related entirely to the establishment clause. Walz's free exercise argument was shunted aside. The opinion said, first, that the law of tax exemption in New York related to many nonprofit agencies including hospitals, libraries, playgrounds, and scientific, historical, and patriotic groups. Such a law had no legislative purpose behind it aimed at establishing or sponsoring or supporting religion. Second, while the exemption provided to the churches did require some interaction or involvement between churches and the state, this involvement was far less extensive than would be the case if churches were subject to the property tax. Exemption ensured less "entanglement" than taxation.

The two concurring opinions defined the meaning of the establishment clause in different ways than did the opinion of the chief justice. And Justice Douglas in dissent argued that tax exemption was an unconstitutional establishment of religion. One case gave us four interpretations of a single clause of the First Amendment from nine judges! [13]

The results? First, New York and forty-nine other states and the federal government did not have to revise their tax laws. Second, Walz and his supporters lost much. The Supreme Court for the first time approved the churches' exemption from the property tax against an establishment of religion challenge. Walz made fully authoritative a position which had been less than that before. Also, the Court almost completely ignored the claim that this tax payment violated Walz's freedom of religion.

But there were other losers too. Some of the groups on the winning side had presented amicus curiae briefs that the Court skipped over. For example: the Baptist Joint Committee on Public Affairs argued that the churches had to be given tax exemption because the free exercise of religion clause required it. Freedom for churches meant no taxation of, at least, houses of worship. The Court ignored this claim just as it had ignored Walz's contrary free religion claim.[14] Pointing out winners and losers in a case concerning the meaning of a constitutionally protected right is not so easy. A person or group might win or lose for reasons it doesn't think are really proper from some theoretical or legal perspective.

A Conclusion

In a democratic society that is divided on the theory of freedom, the law of freedom will probably not completely satisfy all or even most people. The law will remain somewhat ambiguous at crucial points, and that ambiguity will encourage different groups to contend for their preferences if they have the resources and desire for such contention. Again it becomes obvious that eternal vigilance is the price of liberty, even under an excellent Constitution and Bill of Rights.

Notes

[1] West Virginia State Board of Education v. Barnett, 319 U.S. 624 (1943).

[2] Cited in Anson Phelps Stokes and Leo Pfeffer, *Church and State in the United States*, rev. ed. (New York: Harper and Row, 1964), p. 15.

[3] For a scholarly description of these developments see Mark DeWolfe Howe, *The Garden and the Wilderness* (Chicago: Chicago University Press, 1965), chapter 1.

[4] Stokes and Pfeffer, p. 89.

[5] For a more complete study of these matters see Anson Phelps Stokes, *Church and State in the United States*, 3 vol. (New York: Harper and Brothers, 1950). Interestingly, the administration of Jefferson had the phrase, "is not in any sense founded on the Christian religion" omitted from a new version of the treaty with Tripoli ratified in 1805. This change cannot reflect Jefferson's long-held position on the matter. He always argued that Christianity ought not be considered a part of the common law heritage.

[6] Torcaso v. Watkins, 367 U.S. 488 (1961).

[7] Leo Pfeffer, *Church, State and Freedom*, rev. ed. (Boston: Beacon Press, 1967), pp. 241–242.

[8] For the politics of the making of the First Amendment, see Stokes and Pfeffer, pp. 94–100.

[9] For a fine discussion of the Constitutional Convention, equally applicable to the first Congress respecting its work on the First Amendment, see John P. Roche, "The Founding Fathers: A Reform Caucus in Action," 55 *American Political Science Review* 799 (1961).

[10] For a definition of *constitutionalism*, see William G. Andrews, *Constitutions and Constitutionalism* (New York: D. Van Nostrand, 1961), chapter 1.

[11] A book which discusses the activities of groups, religious and secular, with offices in Washington, D.C. that attempt to influence government on the religion clauses of the First Amendment is by Richard E. Morgan, *The Politics of Religious Conflict* (New York: Pegasus, 1968).

[12] Walz v. Tax Commission, 397 U.S. 664 (1970).

[13] For other descriptions of this case, see Leo Pfeffer, *God, Caesar and the Constitution* (Boston; Beacon Press, 1975), pp. 65–81 and Richard E. Morgan, *The Supreme Court and Religion* (New York: The Free Press, 1972), pp. 103–107.

[14] See the magazine of that group, "Baptist Brief Argues for Church Tax Exemption," *Report from the Capital*, November–December, 1969, p. 2.

4
Decisions Supporting
a Claim of Religious Liberty

Introduction

This chapter deals with Supreme Court decisions in which the party demanding freedom won. The next chapter will take up cases in which the freedom claim was lost. Taken together, the subheadings of both chapters give a fairly complete index of religious liberty claims handled by our highest court.

The cases described, plus two already treated in chapters 1 and 3, total over 40 percent of all cases on the free exercise of religion that the Court ever handled.[1] They cover exactly 100 years, 1878 to 1978. It is proper that several cases from the 1940s and several cases pushed by Jehovah's Witnesses should appear. In the 1940s the impact of the Cantwell case, previously discussed, was felt. In it the Supreme Court said that the religious freedom of the First Amendment was included in the Fourteenth Amendment's "due process" clause. This meant that for the first time a person could appeal to the *federal* courts against a *state* limit on that freedom. Since this decision coincided with heightened activity of the aggressive Jehovah's Witnesses, the Supreme Court was presented with religious liberty claims as never before or since.

Also, the sample includes more wins than losses for those demanding liberty. This too reflects what really happened. The United States Supreme Court has been a strong defender of religious freedom since 1940. This indisputable fact needs emphasis.

Surprisingly, the Court has been rather heavily attacked

by the nation's more theologically conservative religious groups. Hopefully, what is said here will impress the reader that these attacks have often been in error. Religious liberty ought to be the most dear of all advantages to the devout. Yet, for the most part their spokespersons have not recognized, let alone praised, the work of the nation's greatest champion of religious liberty—the Supreme Court. Ungrateful beneficiaries of liberty still merit it, for it is theirs by right. But ungrateful beneficiaries of such a precious thing merit criticism as well. How can a people be free if it does not recognize the hand that frees it?

Freedom to Witness in Public Places

Does a person have a constitutional right to make speeches expressing religious beliefs? Yes, undoubtedly. Can a person make such speeches in a public place? Yes, but the state has some power over public places that requires a bit of qualification for the answer. Can a person express religious ideas in any way he or she chooses in a public place without any fear of consequences? No. The state can act against some sorts of expression, but its action must not take effect against a speaker before the speech is made on the supposition that it is dangerous to public order. This seems to be the law developed by the Supreme Court in *Kunz* v. *New York,* 1951.[2] In its decision the Court combined two parts of the First Amendment, freedom of religion and freedom of speech made applicable to the states by the Fourteenth Amendment.

The case concerned an independent Baptist, Reverend Carl Jacob Kunz, director of the "Outdoor Gospel Work" in New York City. He preached on the sidewalks and in the parks to any and all, following, he said, the scriptural mandate to "go out in the highways and hedges" (Luke 14:23). In 1946 he obtained a permit required by city ordinance of all who used public places for such purposes.

When Kunz preached, many people became angry. He said such things as Catholicism was "a religion of the devil," the Pope was "the anti-Christ," and Jews were "Christ killers" who "should have been burnt in the incinerators." These vitriolic comments produced disturbances which Kunz acknowledged occurred, and the police department received strong complaints from many who heard the preaching.

The police commissioner notified Kunz of a hearing that might revoke his permit. At the hearing eighteen complainants appeared, certainly an impressive number. The commissioner revoked the 1946 permit and refused to issue new permits to Kunz in 1947 and 1948. Kunz preached on the sidewalks anyway, and in 1948 he was arrested, tried, convicted, and fined ten dollars. Not one to accept this reprimand, Kunz appealed to the higher courts in New York. He lost at both higher levels. On to the federal Supreme Court he went, aided by the American Civil Liberties Union.

As will be said again and again in the cases that follow, the appellant finally won the case before the United States Supreme Court. The opinion is a good illustration of that Court's overall posture on such a matter. With only one dissent, the Supreme Court overturned, in the name of freedom of religious expression, the decisions of the New York Police Commissioner, the Magistrates Court, the appellate part of the Court of Special Sessions, and the Court of Appeals of New York. Importantly, Chief Justice Vinson, not especially known as a knight vowed to defend liberty, wrote the majority opinion.

The majority gave much weight to the fact that there was "no mention in the ordinance of reasons for which such a permit application can be refused." The police commissioner had no legal guidance on that matter. Rather, he had an unbridled discretion to grant or refuse a permit, according to his pleasure, for unspecified causes.

Equally important was the impact of the refusal to grant the permit. It had force into the future, denying Kunz the right to preach tomorrow and tomorrow, whatever he would then say. Relying on well-established legal decisions respecting freedom of the press, Vinson said that this suppression into the future was an unconstitutional "prior restraint."

These two points were tied together by the Court in a single sentence: "We have here, then, an ordinance which gives an administrative official discretionary power to control in advance the right of citizens to speak on religious matters on the streets."

Therefore, the Court concluded, "the ordinance is clearly invalid as a prior restraint on the exercise of First Amendment rights."

But cannot New York City control its own public places as it chooses? No, said Justice Vinson. Time out of mind, public streets and parks have been places for the communication of ideas and the discussion of public questions. No public officials can change that by a mere administrative decision on the basis of unknown standards.

But what if a sharp-tongued preacher causes a breach of the peace? Must not the city maintain law and order? Yes, there is an obligation to maintain order, but New York has other and ample remedies for breaches of the peace. A person can be arrested, convicted, and punished for that offense. But in the majority view that is not what happened when Kunz applied to renew his permit. "We are here concerned with suppression—not punishment. It is sufficient to say that New York cannot vest restraining control over the right to speak on religious subjects in an administrative official where there are no appropriate standards to guide his action."

One justice did not find it all that clear and simple. Justice Jackson wrote a dissent some four times longer than the majority opinion. It too rested on what courts had said before. It too voiced concern for freedom, but it would have required that Kunz obtain a permit before he addressed audiences on New York streets.

For Justice Jackson the issue was not freedom of religious expression. Kunz was guaranteed that by the Constitution without question. He could speak in a church or rented hall or in any private place as he chose. The issue rather was the alleged right of Kunz to use inflammatory words on the public streets where his audience included passersby who did not want to hear his immoderately phrased message. Some of these poor souls were, in effect, a captive audience of such sidewalk speakers. Did they have to be subjected to harangues? No. Long-established law had always held that "the lewd and obscene, the profane, the libelous, and the insulting or 'fighting' words—those which by their very utterance inflict injury or tend to incite an immediate breach of the peace" could be controlled in a public place.

Jackson thought the Court should look at the big picture. Kunz had once had a permit. He preached. Complaints resulted. A full hearing was held. In it many testified of Kunz's offenses. Kunz conceded that only when a policeman was on hand could he proceed without interruption. The evidence at the hearing, concerning the threat of disorder when Kunz preached, properly resulted in the revocation and denial of permits to Kunz. But Kunz could preach all he wanted away from public places. Order was, therefore, promoted by New York's denial, but freedom was not denied except in the necessary minimal way respecting location.

Perhaps Justice Jackson's dissent was really inspired by what he thought the majority opinion lacked. It gave no verbal formula at all to guide lower courts and administrators as they tried to etch the delicate line between protected freedom and the unprotected abuse of freedom. He suggested the Court might have made reference to the formula Justice Holmes had developed in 1919 in *Schenck* v. *United States*. Then it had been said that speech could be prevented or punished if, he quoted roughly, "the words are used in such circumstances and are of such nature as to create a clear and present danger that they will bring about the substantive evils that the City has a right to prevent."

Whatever one thinks of the dissent, it should be noted that from start to finish of this case only the Supreme Court sided with Kunz. Thus, many state officials and judges, sworn to uphold the Constitution and undoubtedly certain they supported liberty, did not believe Kunz's case was legally sound. And all the judges could cite previous decisions which they said supported their positions. As was said in chapter 3, the law is ambiguous.

Freedom to Witness in Private Places

The zealous person may feel the necessity of reaching people who are not easily reached in order to spread some message. What better way than to knock on doors and speak to those who respond and/or invite them to a meeting? For the Jehovah's Witnesses there is no better way, and Thelma Martin followed it in the city of Struthers, Ohio. Door-to-door she went, passing out an advertisement of a Jehovah's Witness meeting. For this she was arrested, convicted, and fined ten dollars. Her action violated a city law which said, "It is unlawful for any person distributing hand bills, circulars or other advertisements to ring the door bell, sound the knocker, or otherwise summon the inmate or inmates of any residence to the door for the purpose of receiving such . . . (literature)." [3]

Notice, this ordinance is general in that it does not single out religious advertising. Notice also, it is aimed not at those who sell things.

The Supreme Court of the State of Ohio sustained the conviction, and Martin appealed to the federal Supreme Court. The result was *Martin* v. *City of Struthers*, 1943. Hayden C. Covington, whose record of victories before the Court in religious liberty cases was remarkable and unexcelled, argued the Jehovah's Witness cause. He attacked the ordinance as a violation of both freedom of speech and press and of "fundamental personal rights guaranteed against abridgment by the First and Fourteenth Amendment." He did not add the phrase, "freedom of religion," but the case is included in this chapter because it arose out of religious expression.

The Court was sharply divided here, but the majority was vigorously confident that the rights of free speech and press protected Martin from the city ordinance. Justice Black wrote the opinion which stressed that such door-to-door activity was an age-old practice.

There were three elements in the case which needed comparative consideration, he said: the right of the canvasser to spread her ideas, the right of the householder to be informed of those ideas, the power of the state to control an activity that admittedly can be a nuisance and worse. How were these elements to be weighed?

Freedom to distribute information to every citizen wherever he desires to receive it is so clearly vital to the preservation of a free society that, putting aside reasonable police and health regulations of time and manner of distribution, it must be fully preserved. The dangers of distribution can so easily be controlled by traditional legal methods leaving each householder the full right to decide whether he will receive strangers or visitors, that stringent prohibition can serve no purpose but that forbidden by the Constitution, the naked restriction of the dissemination of ideas.

What were these traditional legal methods of controlling a potential nuisance? Between the opinion of Justice Black and the concurring opinion by Justice Murphy, they become clear. The time of canvassing might be reasonably limited. (The city had argued it was trying to preserve the sleep of swing shift workers in war production plants.) The number of canvassers might be limited. Apparently, a registration that ensured their identification would be acceptable. Further, a city might enforce an ordinance which made it illegal to knock on doors where the owner had posted a sign forbidding it.

The law of the city of Struthers, however, was not reasonably designed for these purposes. It did not ensure that people would not be disturbed, as it did not reach the sellers of things. It only ensured that people could not spread or receive materials promoting ideas and advertising meetings. In effect, the city was told to draft its laws more carefully, so that it did not unnecessarily infringe freedom.

The minority opinions stressed the propriety of the city's effort to control a nuisance. A general regulation like that of the city of Struthers was a reasonable means to that end. There must be some limits on freedom. This one was minimal. Said Justice Reed for himself and Justices Jackson and Roberts,

It is impossible for me to discover in this trivial town police regulation a violation of the First Amendment. No ideas are being surpressed. The freedom to teach or preach by word or book is unabridged, save only the right to call a householder to the door of his house to receive the summoner's message. I cannot expand this regulation to a violation of the First Amendment.

The dissent is forceful. After all, there are many ways to spread ideas and give notice of meetings. Had the minority prevailed, Martin could have scarcely complained that free expression was lost. Just one form of it.

However, the majority properly noted that people with little money would be seriously affected if such ordinances became common. Door-to-door visits are cheaper, and often more effective, than most commercial means of advertising. Thus, the victory of Martin was an important civil liberties victory for "little people."

Freedom to Sell Literature Door-to-Door

Numbers may tell little about the difficulty of deciding a case, but when the vote in two similar cases totals out at nine to nine in two year's time, the case must be treated as a difficult one. Those were the totals in *Jones* v. *Opelika*, 1942, and *Murdock* v. *Pennsylvania*, 1943.[4]

In each of these cases the issue was the same: Could a locality's license fee on all door-to-door peddlers be charged to those who conducted evangelism through sales of religious literature? In 1942 the license fee was upheld five to four. In 1943 it was struck down five to four. No judge changed his mind. But Justice Brynes left the Court, being replaced by Justice Rutledge. Thus, in spite of slogans which speak of being ruled by law, not men, even in our courts we are ruled by men—at least when the issues are closely drawn.

Since in *Murdock* v. *Pennsylvania* the new majority felt it had to answer the arguments of the old majority, we can get at all the issues by concentrating on it.

The city of Jeanette, Pennsylvania, had a long-standing ordinance requiring a license of those who sold anything door-to-door. Its rates were modest, applying equally to all sorts of canvassers. Murdock, one of several similar plaintiffs, was a Jehovah's Witness. He regularly went door-to-door talking about his religious beliefs and "selling" religious literature. The prices charged were only suggested prices, any contribution for the literature would do. Indeed, to some it was given free. Murdock refused to get a license on grounds that the city requirement deprived him of freedom of religion. He was arrested, convicted, and fined. He appealed through Pennsylvania courts but lost. On to the Supreme Court he went. There he too was supported by the attorney of the Witnesses, Hayden C. Covington.[5]

Justice Douglas wrote the majority opinion, beginning in decisive fashion. "It could hardly be denied that a tax laid specifically on the exercise of . . . (religion) would be unconstitutional. Yet the license tax imposed by this ordinance is in substance just that."

Why so? Because for the obviously sincere Witnesses their religion compelled them to teach "publickly, and from house to house" (Acts 20:20). This form of evangelism to these earnest people was what a regular worship service would be to adherents of more traditional religions.

To Douglas the record made it plain that their activity was primarily religious rather than primarily commercial. The mere fact that money was raised in this way did not in and of itself make the activity commercial. If it did, "The passing of the collection plate in a church would make the church service a commercial project."

Did this mean that no tax could be applied to churches

or clergymen? No. The tax being considered hit directly at religious expression. Therefore, the decision would not include taxes that did not operate in this forbidden way. Justice Douglas gave examples: an income tax on a clergyman's earnings and a tax on church property would not be covered by his narrowly defined terms.

The opinion noted that arguments made in the court concerning the irritation that Jehovah's Witnesses caused as they went about their evangelism were irrelevant. So were arguments which said that the city had an interest in controlling fraud and other unlawful acts perpetrated by canvassers and those posing as such. The city could handle those problems by a carefully drawn ordinance aimed at abuses, not by a general tax that reached religious activities.

The minority, echoing the earlier majority opinion in the Jones case, found that the Witnesses were involved in a commercial enterprise when they "sold" literature. Since the city could tax any local commercial enterprise and since the tax did not discriminate against those who sold religious materials, the ordinance was quite constitutional.

One year later in *Follett* v. *Town of McCormick* the Supreme Court applied its Murdock opinion to a person who made his whole livelihood from door-to-door sales of Bibles and other religious literature. It reasoned in a similar fashion. For Follett, selling this literature was a mode of religious expression. Just as a clergyman could not be taxed for conducting worship, so a salesman whose selling was a religious act could not be taxed for that act.[6]

Thus by 1944, a specific activity that the Supreme Court could decide was religious had been given tax exemption on grounds of the free exercise of religion. Of course, someone might fret that once this had been decided unscrupulous people would call almost any action religious in order to avoid some tax. From Justice Douglas' opinion in Murdock, it was clear that he believed that courts were wise enough to handle that matter if it arose. And so they are—usually.

Freedom from Patriotic Exercises

The heading for this section might well be disputed by the families of Walter Barnette, Paul Stull, and Lucy McClure. Given their religious beliefs, it would better be called, "Freedom from Forced Idolatry." They had gone to a federal district court for an order to stop enforcement of a West Virginia law that required public school pupils to join in a flag salute. To them the salute ceremony was idolatry. The result was the landmark decision of *West Virginia State Board of Education* v. *Barnette*.[7]

Notice the order of names in the case tells us that West Virginia officials had appealed to the Supreme Court. They had lost in a special three-judge district court. To some, the loss there was a surprise, for only three years earlier the Supreme Court had decided an identical case by a whopping eight to one majority in favor of school authorities. The loss may seem a surprise for another reason. The United States was at war with Germany, Japan, and Italy. It was the day for enthusiastic patriotism. It was the time when the rights of some—Japanese-Americans—were overridden roughshod.

Yet, a lowly federal district court boldly decided that it should over rule the earlier Supreme Court decision of *Minersville School District* v. *Gobitis*.[8] Why? There were at least four reasons: First, the Supreme Court seemed changed. In the 1942 Opelika decision concerning a city license fee on peddlers of religious literature, the majority referred to the Gobitis decision in a way which questioned its validity. More importantly, the minority in that case included three justices, Black, Murphy, and Douglas, who apologized for their Gobitis votes saying, "It was wrongly decided." [9] These three, plus Justice Stone, who had been the lone Gobitis dissenter, totaled four judges willing to overrule the earlier decision on required flag salutes. And two other justices, Jackson and Rutledge, had been appointed since the Gobitis verdict.

A second reason for the district court's boldness was that

the Gobitis decision had been much criticized in both popular and learned writing. It had also received support in the nation's presses, but the negative criticism had been quite sharp and effectively argued.

Third, a new federal law had been passed on flag observances. Public Law 623 said that "full respect" could be given during salute ceremonies "by merely standing at attention, men removing the headdress." While this was a federal law and the practices contested by Barnette involved a state statute, the new law seemed like an authoritative pronouncement that should be accepted by all.

Fourth, many people were deeply shocked at the alarming persecution in all sections of the nation of Jehovah's Witnesses. The persecution seemed related to their refusal to join in flag salutes, and it mounted after the Gobitis opinion was handed down. Since few people now remember this ugly episode of our history, a brief note of it is unpleasantly necessary.

While Jehovah's Witnesses had received rough treatment in some places for years, after June of 1940, when the Court approved the flag salute requirement, an incredible series of events occurred. In Maine there were beatings, a Witness Kingdom Hall was sacked and burned, six Witnesses who used shotgun fire against a crowd of people throwing rocks at them were charged with attempted murder. In Illinois a whole small town attacked a caravan of Witnesses' cars, overturning and burning some of them. The Witnesses, both men and women, were beaten by the crowd. In a Wyoming city a man was tarred and feathered. In Mississippi an American Legion-led crowd forcefully escorted some cars and trailers of Witnesses who had assembled for a convention to the state line of Louisiana. There separate groups of legionnaires escorted them from county to county on to Texas. In Texas the process was continued until at Dallas the forced traveling was finally ended. In Nebraska a member of the sect was abducted and castrated. In Arkansas pipeline workers invaded a Witness convention and beat all the poor souls they could find. In Oregon a mob of 1,000 stormed a Kingdom Hall. Maryland police joined a mob that broke up a Witness meeting. In West Virginia a deputy sheriff tied up a group of Witnesses, forced them to drink large amounts of castor oil, and marched them out of town. Arrests were made in many other places on a variety of charges, many unjustified on any ground.

Happily, there was something of a national reaction to these atrocities. The reaction called into question the desirability of compulsory flag salute, for it was the Witnesses' refusal to salute the flag more than anything else that seemed to spur the persecution.[10]

When the district court held against West Virginia and for the children who refused to salute the flag, the state appealed to the Supreme Court. The state argued simply that the Gobitis case was identical. It had settled the matter. Therefore, the West Virginia regulation was valid. In this argument the state was supported by a similar amicus curiae brief filed by the American Legion.

Again attorney Hayden C. Covington made the case for the Witnesses. His attack on the salute rule was mounted from several directions. He argued that it violated freedom of speech, worship, conscience, and freedom of parents to direct the spiritual lives of their children. In his general thrust he was supported by amicus curiae briefs of the American Bar Association and the American Civil Liberties Union. In combination, and in much abbreviated and highly selected form, the arguments for the Witnesses included these points.

First, freedom of religion and conscience was at issue because the Witnesses' children believed it an unforgivable sin to violate the Commandment found in Exodus 20 against the worship of a graven image. The salute of the flag was for them a religious ceremony involving this forbidden worship—an act of idolatry. Such an act by a Witness ensured eternal punishment.

Second, freedom of speech was at issue because state law enforcing the salute required expulsion for those who refused.

Expulsion meant nonattendance. That meant legal truancy. That meant legal delinquency. Thus, the state was attempting to coerce the salute out of unwilling mouths.

Third, since the Supreme Court had held in free expression cases that only a clear and present danger to the nation's interest warranted a limitation on free speech and press, it should restrain West Virginia from enforcing its law. Obviously, the mere silence of a few Witness children, who were willing to stand quietly during the salute, created no such danger. Their's was an act of omission of no consequence to the state, not an act of commission causing injury to anyone or to the nation's well-being.

Justice Jackson, who had not been on the Court when the Gobitis decision had been handed down, wrote the majority opinion. It was supported by five other justices, three of whom had shifted positions since the earlier case.

Jackson noted that federal laws related to the flag salute and to conscientious objectors made room for people whose consciences differed from the national norm. For reasons not explained, he said, local officials were less sensitive to constitutional limits on power than their federal counterparts.

But were not these local officials democratically elected? Could the people not rule through them, even if they were insensitive to rights? No, was Jackson's answer. "The very purpose of the Bill of Rights was to withdraw certain subjects from the vicissitudes of political controversy, to place them beyond the reach of majorities and officials and to establish them as legal principles to be applied by the courts. One's right to life, liberty, and property, to free speech, a free press, freedom of worship and assembly, and other fundamental rights may not be submitted to vote; they depend on the outcome of no election."

But could the state not promote unity by education of the young in this way? No. Such education was destructive of unity.

As governmental pressure toward unity becomes greater, so strife becomes more bitter as to whose unity it shall be. Probably no deeper division of our people could proceed from any provocation than from finding it necessary to choose what doctrine and whose program public educational officials shall compel youth to unite in embracing. Ultimate futility of such attempts to compel coherence is the lesson of every such effort from the Roman drive to stamp out Christianity as a disturber of its pagan unity, the Inquisition, as a means to religious and dynastic unity, the Siberian exiles as a means to Russian unity, down to the fast failing efforts of our present totalitarian enemies. Those who begin coercive elimination of dissent soon find themselves exterminating dissenters. Compulsory unification of opinion achieves only the unanimity of the graveyard. It seems trite but necessary to say that the First Amendment to our Constitution was designed to avoid these ends by avoiding these beginnings.

And then the eloquent conclusion. "If there is any fixed star in our constitutional constellation, it is that no official, high or petty, can prescribe what shall be orthodox in politics, nationalism, religion, or other matters of opinion, or force citizens to confess by word or act their faith therein." Freedom has seldom enjoyed a better defense.

While Justices Reed and Roberts noted their objection by reference to the majority opinion in Gobitis, Justice Frankfurter developed a long dissent. In it he lectured his black-robed brethren at tedious length on the need for judicial self-restraint. "Let the elected officials decide," is a good paraphrase of his thrust. The Supreme Court, he thought, was ill-prepared to replace locally elected school boards as the education authority of the nation.

Should the Court not defend constitutional rights as Justice Jackson had urged for the majority? Part of Justice Frankfurter's answer included these ideas: the children were only required to participate, not to believe what the ceremony and words say. And parents did not have to send children to public schools; any approved private school would do.

Here Justice Frankfurter was making an argument that could not be easily related to reality. The Witnesses were either too sincere or not diabolically sophisticated enough to join in the salute and not mean it. As to the second point, they were too few and scattered to operate their own schools given their relative poverty. The justice was only arguing, not thinking constructively. But, of course, he had written the now over-turned decision in the Gobitis case just three years earlier.

Happily for America, the issue was all but settled by the decision. Local school boards generally complied swiftly. And Americans, busy with the dramatic offensives of World War II, ended their senseless persecutions, with minor exceptions.

An almost whimsical echo of the flag salute cases was heard in 1977, however, reminding us that such issues never really disappear. It involved a New Hampshire motto embossed on auto license plates which read, "Live Free or Die." Two Jehovah's Witnesses, George and Maxine Maynard covered up the motto, because they found it offensive on religious and moral grounds. (Remember, the Witnesses hold to a special kind of pacificism.) When George Maynard was arrested for obscuring lettering on the plate, the couple went to federal district court asking for an order against the application of the offensive law. They won an injunction against its enforcement, and the state appealed. In *Wooley* v. *Maynard,* Justice Burger, for a majority of six, sided with the two Witnesses. He argued that requiring them to use the motto invaded their First Amendment rights and that their action in covering the motto did not adversely affect any state interest.[11] Neither by words required of us nor by mottoes forced upon our cars must we attest to some governmental creed.

Freedom to and from Education

The state has a high interest in the education of children. So do churches. So do religious people. So do children. Inevitably, legal conflicts arise as these groups and people take action concerning their interests. The Supreme Court has handed down several rulings on these conflicts.

The first of these, *Pierce* v. *Society of Sisters,* 1925, concerned an Oregon law passed by a statewide petition and referendum of the voters.[12] The law required attendance of all children at public schools. Its operation was designed to destroy parochial education. Bluntly put, the law was anti-Catholic.

Unhappily, from today's perspective, the Supreme Court decision which found the law unconstitutional is a poor one. Rather than being grounded squarely on the free exercise of religion clause, the Court grounded its work on the rights of property. Why? Because the state law was challenged by the owners of two private schools—the Society of Sisters and the Hill Military Academy. They both went to federal district court asserting that the Oregon statute deprived them of their valuable property without due process of law. Thus, the law violated the Fourteenth Amendment's property clause.

Why didn't the Catholic Society of Sisters push their claim on grounds of religious freedom? Why didn't the parents of a child in a religious school do the same? Because in 1923, when the case started, the Supreme Court had not yet held that First Amendment rights, aimed at the federal government, were applicable to the states by the broad words of the Fourteenth Amendment. That application, as noted above, was begun later. Further, in the first three decades of this century, it was relatively easy to win property cases against the several states in federal courts.

So, the only case we have on the right of religious groups to operate schools and the right of religious people to attend them is curiously bottomed on property consideration rather than religious ones. Undoubtedly, if the same case were to arise today, it would be treated by lawyers and judges as a case concerned with parental and religious freedom. Indeed, the majority opinion even then wandered off its theme of property rights into a legally irrelevant discussion of rights in general. Justice Reynolds, a staunch conservative who was at home with property rights, threw in this broad paragraph for good measure.

> We think it entirely plain that the Act of 1922 unreasonably interferes with the liberty of parents . . . to direct the upbringing and education of children . . . (R)ights guaranteed by the Constitution may not be abridged by legislation which has no reasonable relation to some purpose within the competency of the state. The fundamental theory of liberty upon which all governments of the Union repose excludes any general power of the state to standardize its children by forcing them to accept instruction from public teachers only. The child is no mere creature of the state; those who nurture him and direct his destiny have the right, coupled with the high duty, to recognize and prepare him for additional obligation.

The Court specified in its opinion that the state could regulate and inspect private schools in a reasonable way to ensure that the education offered was adequate to meet the state's interests in education. And state laws generally place requirements on private schools that serve as alternatives to public schools.[13] Thus, the operation of private and parochial schools comes under some state regulation.

What if parents claimed as a religious right that they ought *not* be required to send their children to school at all? This was the argument of some parents in the case of *Wisconsin* v. *Yoder*, 1972.[14] They were members of the very conservative (perhaps, radical) Old Order Amish who farm for a living, wear eighteenth-century clothing, use no automobiles or electricity, and in general, renounce most of what they see in the outside world.

The Amish parents refused to send their children, ages fourteen and fifteen, to public schools. Neither did they send them to any other school. They were charged, tried, and convicted of violating Wisconsin's school attendance law. Each was fined five dollars by the county court. The parents appealed their conviction up the state judicial ladder, losing in the circuit court but winning in the state supreme court. Then Wisconsin applied to the federal Supreme Court, which granted a full hearing.

The lawyers for the parents argued as follows: The long-practiced Amish faith required that its followers live a life characterized by simplicity, hard work, noncompetiveness, and by a sharp separation from the world and worldly influences. The ideal was the life-style of the early Christians as the Amish understood it. In pursuit of their life-style parents agreed that an elementary education was necessary so that their children would learn the three R's. Reading the Bible was an especially useful skill. This basic education was needed within the Amish community and in the necessary dealings the Amish had with the outside world. Such a limited formal learning in the child's younger years was not destructive of Amish faith and life. However, by the time the child went beyond the eighth grade, formal education required by the state was inappropriate to Amish needs and destructive of Amish beliefs and ways. Therefore, as a matter of religious belief, the parents refused to allow school attendance beyond the eighth grade. Of course, the Amish child was taught practical skills at home by an effective but informal education.

Wisconsin countered with the assertion that the power of the state over education was settled and that the rule requiring attendance to age sixteen was reasonable. Many states had it. The state had to ensure that it had an educated citizenry in light of twentieth-century needs in order to promote the economic well-being of each and all and in order to promote intelligent democratic participation in government. Further, the state had to promote the welfare of children even against the wishes of parents. After all, some Amish children left the simple religious community and made their way in the larger society. The state had to aid these.

The Supreme Court found itself forced to weigh against each other the sincere religious beliefs of Amish parents and the admitted educational powers and interests of the state. It concluded that neither was absolute. One must be balanced against the other, and one must prevail given the facts of the case.

The Court noted that the Amish people could point to some three hundred years of continuous history as unique communities, that they were successful in providing jobs and security for their members, rejecting governmental welfare programs, that they gave all their children a sort of on-the-job education in the skills their communities and the world-at-large needed, and that this education was apparently more effective than what the public schools could offer.

Therefore, the Supreme Court concluded that, *given the facts of this case,* the state had not demonstrated that its requirement of school attendance should outweigh the deep religious faith and life-style of the parents. It affirmed the Wisconsin high court's decision, reversing the county court convictions.

At several points Chief Justice Burger's opinion went out of its way to stress that the Court was here considering the religion of a long-established and successful sect. The Court, he said, was only concerned with religious beliefs and that these were the only beliefs that the First Amendment specified. Also, he distinguished religious beliefs from personal and philosophic beliefs in a way which tended to give a narrow definition to religion. Why was the chief justice so cautious?

The opinion was narrowly drawn because the Court was obviously worried about other communities in the society. It did not want to give every hippie commune the right to keep their children out of school. One expert critic of the Supreme Court, picking up this problem, wrote an article about the case entitled, "The Importance of Being Amish." [15]

What was at issue here if the Court became too specific about whose beliefs permitted such an exception to state laws was this: Would not a special legal concern for any religious group's rights give that group a preference in law? If so, was the preference not an "establishment of religion," which violated the establishment clause of the First Amendment?

Justice Douglas alone dissented in a qualified way. He worried that the Court had defined religion too narrowly. For him, religion was any belief that influenced the person in the same way as did a traditional religious belief. Here he followed what the Court had said about religious belief in the conscientious objector cases. Also, he worried about the rights of the Amish child. He found in the lower court record that only one child of the families involved had testified that her religious beliefs were like her parents on the matter of school attendance. Justice Douglas said this assured him that for that family the decision was proper. But since no other child had so testified, Justice Douglas wanted the case returned to the lower court to find if the other children involved agreed with their parents.

Thus, Justice Douglas wanted this to be a case which would handle the claims of three parties: child, parent, and state. He almost implied that a child's rights to a formal education, if the child wanted one, would be superior to the parental religious demand not to have the child so educated.

Reading both the majority and minority opinions, it is clear that the court would concern itself with the rights of children in a similar case if these rights were clearly raised. This will make the Supreme Court's balancing requirement more difficult. Not only are three considerations more difficult to balance than two, but the rights of children are less easily identified and defined than the rights of parents or the power of the state. Are the rights of a seventeen-year-old as valid against the parents as the rights of a seven-year-old? Not for all purposes. Our courts have only begun to develop this area of the law of rights.

Freedom from Government Discrimination

For people interested in religious liberty, the case o *Sherbert* v. *Verner,* 1963, is still as important as any for severa reasons: [16] The opinion was generous respecting the free exer cise clause. The opinion set to rest, for a time at least, an olde and rather restrictive view of what religious freedom meant

Also, the justices were forced by the facts of the case to ask how the free exercise clause and the antiestablishment clause were related. Here are those facts.

Adell Sherbert, a Seventh-Day Adventist, was discharged from her job in a textile mill because she had refused to work on Saturday, her sabbath. Applying for similar work in other mills, she was turned down for the same reason. Then she applied to the state for unemployment compensation. The South Carolina Employment Security Commission refused her application. By law the unemployed were eligible for state aid only if they accepted "suitable work when offered." This, Sherbert had not done. Her religious scruples were not an adequate excuse for rejecting work in the commission's view. She appealed to the state courts, losing at all levels. Up to the federal Supreme Court she went. It heard the case and decided in her favor, overturning the state decisions. Why?

Justice Brennan found that the issue was squarely a matter of the free exercise of religion. The state's unemployment insurance law directly interfered with that exercise. Against her conscience, it pressured her to take Saturday work. It was almost as if the government fined those who worshiped on Saturday.

Brennan found previous cases in which the Supreme Court had said that the states could not put special conditions upon public benefits if those conditions operated to limit First Amendment freedoms. Also, he showed that other South Carolina employment laws made special allowance for those who would not work on *Sunday* because of conscience. Since the state had made that allowance, it could not discriminate against Sabbatarians.

Then he asked if there was some "compelling state interest" which the statute in question protected? He found none. What of the state's contention that if it made an exception for people like Sherbert, there might be fraudulent claims by the unscrupulous, feigning religious objections to Saturday work? Such claims, the state argued, would both cost it money and hinder employers from scheduling Saturday work.

To Brennan this argument was not effective. First, a technical legal matter was at issue. The state had not raised this issue in its own courts where it could be more properly weighed. Second, nothing in the record of the case indicated that the contention was more than hypothetical. What facts made it important?

Here Brennan was trying to distinguish the facts at issue from those presented in four cases concerning Sunday closing laws decided only two years earlier.[17] In those cases the same Court had held that people who closed their businesses on Saturday for religious reasons could also be forced by law to close them on Sunday. Admitting that such people were seriously affected by these blue laws, the Court, nevertheless, decided that the state had a "compelling interest" in them. That interest was the secular—not religious—concern to provide a rest day each week for workers. A common rest day promoted the general welfare in a variety of ways.

The justice's opinion also distinguished Sherbert's situation from those forced to close their businesses on Sunday in another way. True, both were hurt by state power. However, the impact of South Carolina's law on Sherbert was more direct—she lost a regular, fixed compensation from the state—while the impact of Sunday closing laws was less direct—businessmen lost an uncertain amount of Sunday sales. Thus, the decision protecting Sherbert could be different from the previous decision which had not protected those forced to close their businesses on Sunday.

Justices Douglas and Stewart concurred separately with Brennan. But they would have flatly overruled the Sunday closing cases as being wrongly decided. They were pleased the Court had at last seen the light but sorry it did not publicly repent of its earlier sin against Sabbatarians.

Justices Harlan and White dissented. To them the state's reasonable and purely secular law should not be struck down because some person's conscience prohibited their benefiting from it. South Carolina treated all alike, whatever the reason for their not being able to work. Now the majority opinion would force South Carolina to give a special break to those who could not work on Saturday for religious reasons. Sherbert, by reason of her conscience, would henceforth get unemployment compensation; another person, who could not work Saturdays because, for example, no baby-sitter was available, would not. To the minority this was an improper state discrimination of the basis of religion—that is, a sort of establishment of one religion.

Justice Brennan had dismissed this problematic issue by briefly noting that state unemployment payments would "not represent that involvement of religious with secular institutions which it is the object of the Establishment Clause to forestall."

This part of the majority opinion seemed far too brief for some people. Clearly, there is a problem when a state must accept a religious excuse for not working over a nonreligious excuse. Had Justice Brennan wrestled more seriously with this problem, his opinion might well have been less subject to criticism.

Freedom for Churches to Control Their Affairs

For most people, it would seem obvious that churches ought to be able to control their own affairs. So they ought. But, alas, who is the church must be a matter for the state to decide in some cases. Why? Because churches split and squabble over those things in which the state has a concern. When two rival church factions contest the ownership of property, one of them may appeal to the state to settle the issue. The state, after all, exists in part to determine who owns property.

A rather recent case, *Presbyterian Church in the United States* v. *Mary Elizabeth Blue Hull Memorial Presbyterian Church* will serve as an excellent example of how courts get involved in intrachurch property conflicts,[18] but this kind of dispute is now new in American legal history. Such cases were especially common in New England state courts in the early nineteenth century when Unitarian majorities of the town took over churches to the hurt and righteous indignation of Trinitarian minorities.[19] Remember, slow-changing Massachusetts had a form of religious establishment until 1833, and, therefore, qualified state voters could vote on church business. Then, and in a federal court decision involving a church split in Kentucky over Civil War issues,[20] most courts decided that they could not judge the theological issues at stake. Rather, the courts handled the cases purely as property matters, determining ownership on the basis of how the church itself claimed to govern its own affairs. That is, the court would handle such disputes the way it handled disputes over the ownership of any corporation's property. This is how the Supreme Court handled the case at issue here.

In Chatham County, Georgia, two local Presbyterian churches voted to withdraw from the denomination with which they were affiliated—the Presbyterian Church in the United States. They did so because, they said, the denomination had departed from its original religious doctrines and tenets. Their purpose was to continue as local churches true to the traditional Presbyterian faith. The denomination sought to conciliate this intrachurch dispute by use of a special church commission set up by the regional Presbytery of Savannah. Each local church majority remained steadfast in its decision to withdraw, and the commission took over the local churches' properties pending the time new local leadership could be appointed.

The local church leaders did not appeal the commission's action to higher church officers—a thing which Presbyterian procedures call for in conflicts like this. Rather, the local churches filed suits in the county court to stop the denomination from trespassing on the properties. The denomination moved in the court to dismiss this action. It also filed a suit to stop the local groups from using the properties.

The county judge submitted the case to the jury, telling it to decide whether the Presbyterian Church in the United States had departed from its original doctrines. That is, the jurors were told to decide a theological question. The jury decided that the denomination had indeed departed from the true Presbyterian faith of the past, and, therefore, the trial judge held that an "implied trust" between the denomination and the local churches had been broken. This meant that the faithful local churches could claim the properties. The county court's action was upheld by the Supreme Court of Georgia. The denomination appealed to the United States Supreme Court. That court granted a full hearing. What did it decide?

The Supreme Court had little difficulty, it seems, in reaching the decision to overrule the state courts. It referred in the majority opinion of Justice Brennan to three earlier cases all pointing in the same direction. All had found the secular courts incompetent in light of the First Amendment's religion clauses to handle disputes over church doctrine, because, quoting a decision of 1872:

In this country the full and free right to entertain any religious belief, to practice any religious principle, and to teach any religious doctrine which does not violate the laws of morality and property, and which does not infringe personal rights, is conceeded to all. The law knows no heresy, and is committed to the support of no dogma, the establishment of no sect . . . All who unite themselves to such a body . . . (the denomination) do so with the implied consent to (its) government, and are bound to submit to it. But it would be a vain consent and would lead to the total subversion of such religious bodies, if anyone aggrieved by one of their decisions could appeal to the secular courts and have (those decisions) reversed. It is of the essence of these religious unions, and of their right to establish tribunals for the decision of questions arising among themselves, that those decisions should be binding in all cases of ecclesiastical cognizance, subject only to such appeals as the organization itself provides for.

This meant that the local churches in this case should have appealed their dispute from—given Presbyterian structure—the local church session, to the regional presbytery, to the state-wide synod, to the national general assembly—not to secular courts. Those Presbyterian agencies alone could decide a doctrinal dispute within Presbyterian churches. Each denomination, then, is the only structure that can properly settle a theological dispute within that denomination, even if it concerns such a worldly matter as the ownership of property. So, in a denomination like the American or Southern Baptists, which has final power located in the local congregation, there would be no appeal beyond the local congregation's business meeting on a local property conflict.

But there is a qualification that must be especially noted. If the complaining party asserts that there was within the church or denomination "fraud, collusion, or arbitrariness" in the procedure or the meeting which finally settled the dispute, the secular courts will listen to the complaint and may intervene to ensure that procedures are fair. For example, suppose that a crucial business meeting concerning a dispute were called and that no notice of the meeting was given to one of the factions. Then, the secular courts would act to require proper notice.

In brief, the First Amendment's demand for religious freedom ensures that churches and denominations can settle their disputes over doctrine themselves by their own processes. The secular courts will upset their decisions on such matters only if it can be shown that some party to an intrachurch dispute rigged the process improperly or unfairly according to the denomination's own rules. The secular courts have no religious duties respecting churches, but they do have duties to protect any church member or faction from intrachurch fraud.

Justice Harlan in a concurring opinion said he agreed fully with the opinion but wanted to add a further qualification. The secular courts could enforce "a deed or will which expressly and clearly lays down conditions limiting a religious organization's use of the property which is granted. If, for example, the donor expressly gives his church some money on the condition that the church never ordain a woman . . . or never amend certain specified articles of the Confession of Faith, he is entitled to his money back if the condition is not fulfilled."

Notice that Justice Harlan's examples involve express and clear terms that any court would have little trouble handling. His qualification may not be a major one. He too leaves doctrinal disputes up to church governments for settlement.

Whatever the merits of this decision, one thing is clear. It was the two church factions that appealed to a court to intervene. If the church groups had chosen, they could have managed the matter by their own processes. This they were free to do under law. But when the two factions tried to use state power to secure the property, the state had to ask how its laws on property should be applied.

Here, the Supreme Court's application of property law clearly benefits any denomination which has a centralized structure for settling such matters. One must assume that the centralized structure's committees or tribunals will usually side with the denomination against some local faction. But for denominations that have all power centered in the local congregation, the Supreme Court's decision benefits those people who can round up a bare majority at a properly called business meeting. For some such denominations, this has meant that the central offices are very careful when they loan money or give financial support to local congregations. They hire lawyers to draft agreements to ensure that no bare majority on some conflict-filled night can pull out of the denomination with all the local property. Clearly, the government's laws on property and on the operation of private associations affect church affairs. Can it be otherwise when churches split and wrangle over who owns what and who perpetrated which fraud?

Freedom of Religion in Prison

Can prisoners claim religious freedom? Not long ago the answer was an unqualified no. Today the answer is a qualified yes. The change was part of a broader change in the ways courts treated the constitutional pleas of the "lawfully incarcerated."

Until the 1940s, with rarest exception, state and federal

courts alike held that prisoners were without constitutional rights of any sort. They were "slaves of the state." Having been found guilty by due process of law and having had that guilt confirmed by regular posttrial appeals, prisoners could thereafter only ask for mercy from the state. They could not make a constitutional demand upon it concerning the quality of prison life.

This dismal legal situation led to ugly prison abuses across the nation, and since the 1940s the courts have shown an increasing willingness to move against state and federal prison practices. The changed attitude of the courts has given prisoners the right of access to the courts, to legal counsel, and to legal materials. Further, now it is possible to claim the right to communicate with society beyond the walls and to have protection from cruel and unusual punishments. But what about the right to religious freedom? [21]

Today religious freedom leaps prison walls, but it does so in a sharply crippled form. For example, courts have held that there is no right to attend prison worship services for prisoners held in solitary confinement or even for dangerous inmates held under maximum security. Nor is there a right to mail Christmas cards without normal prison censorship. A non-Jew does not have the right to attend Jewish services. Also, only in the last decade, and with great caution, have the courts been willing to question the assumption of prison officials that the followers of the Black Muslim faith could not be permitted to practice most aspects of their religion. In the typical warden's eyes, these prisoners always pose too dire a threat to prison safety and security. [22]

Inevitably as lower courts began to make these changes, the Supreme Court was presented with prisoner rights appeals. One of these related to freedom of religion, *Cruz* v. *Beto,* 1972. [23] The Court's per curiam opinion was at once clear but too short to be thorough. Yet, it is as authoritative as any opinion that exists on the subject. (Per curiam opinions are usually very brief and always unsigned by the author.)

Fred A. Cruz, asserting that he and others in a Texas prison were Buddhists, claimed that they were not permitted to use the prison chapel, to freely exchange Buddhist literature and to correspond with religious advisors. Also, he noted that Protestants, Catholics, and Jews alone had chaplains and Scriptures paid for by the state. Further, prisoners who practiced one of those three faiths received merit points for their goodness, while Buddhists did not. The merit points were useful in helping obtain preferred prison jobs and early parole.

The Federal District Court and the Court of Appeals denied relief without a hearing or any findings, the former asserting that such matters should be left "to the sound discretion of prison administrators." The phrase, it should be noted, was a traditional one that courts had always used when summarily denying prisoners' claims against prison officials. It added, "valid disciplinary and security reasons not known to this court may prevent the 'equality' of exercise of religious practices in prison."

But the Supreme Court took the position that such an assumption was not justifiable without a full hearing. It said in part,

Federal courts sit not to supervise prisons but to enforce the constitutional rights of all "persons," including prisoners. We are not unmindful that prison officials must be accorded latitude in the administration of prison affairs, and that prisoners necessarily are subject to appropriate rules . . . But persons in prison . . . have the right to petition the Government for redress of grievances which, of course, includes "access of prisoners to the courts for the purpose of presenting their complaints."

If Cruz was a Buddhist and if he was denied a reasonable opportunity of preserving his faith comparable to . . . fellow prisoners . . . , then there was palpable discrimination by the State against the Buddhist religion . . . The First Amendment applicable to the State by reason of the Fourteenth Amendment . . . prohibits government from making a law "prohibiting the free exercise of religion."

In a footnote the opinion added that the Court was not suggesting that every sect, however few its members, need be given identical facilities and personnel for its religious practices. Chief Justice Burger felt so strongly about this point that he wrote a separate concurring opinion of one paragraph stressing it.

Justice Rehnquist's dissent reflected a wariness and weariness of prisoners' petitions. He would give broad discretion to district courts to dismiss these often, obviously "frivolous and malicious" complaints without a hearing. Further, he believed that this prisoner's complaint may have been fully litigated before.

The dissent puts its finger on a major problem for the courts respecting prisoners' appeals. Now that the right of access to the courts is available, a large number of applications from prisoners are filed regularly. Many are completely without legal merit. Many are flatly false. Some judges may believe they can identify these from the original petition and from the prison's official response. Thus it is unnecessary to waste time and money on the absurd.

The difficulty with that position is this: Some very unprofessional prisoners' complaints have contained some truth. How can these be sorted out without a full hearing? For some problems of freedom there is no easy and cheap solution.

One knotty issue raised by the demand for freedom of religion in prisons is related to the establishment clause. Since courts have said that state monetary aids for, or excessive state entanglements with, religious agencies are forbidden under the establishment clause, can the government make any provision for religion in prisons or, for that matter, in the military and in state hospitals? To the limited extent courts have wrestled with that question the answer shapes up as follows. When the state puts people in places where normal religious expression is prohibited without some state aid and cooperation, the state must provide that aid and cooperation.[24] That is, the requirement of the "free exercise" clause of the First Amendment may in some cases overrule the standards of the antiestablishment clause. Otherwise, some people would be denied the right to practice their faith because the government had control over their lives in a special way.

Freedom from the Military Draft

At the beginning of this section one point must be strongly stressed. With rare exception, *courts have not held that the free exercise of religion guarantee of the First Amendment shields anyone from the draft law. There is no right to be a conscientious objector in the constitutional sense.* There never has been.

On what then does the conscientious objector rely? Only on the law passed by Congress. Congress grants the exemption as a matter of its free choice. Congress could eliminate that exemption tomorrow if it wished. Put differently, conscientious objector status is a matter of congressional grace, not of constitutional right. The same is true of military deferments given to ministers and seminary students.

This means, of course, that Congress has power to control all aspects of the draft law. Among other things, it can require registration and set punishments for those who fail to register, even if it is claimed that the failure is an act of conscience. It can define the meaning of such terms as *conscientious objector* and *minister* pretty much as it chooses, even if the definitions do not suit the needs of all persons or sects. It can require noncombatant or alternative service of all objectors. Because of the rigidity of draft law definitions in World War II, about one in every six inmates of federal prisons by 1945 was a conscientious objector to war.

Yet, a glance at history will show that both administrators and the courts have whittled away at the sweeping power of Congress "to raise and support armies," in part because they were sensitive to the spirit of the First Amendment. As a result, congressional power to establish a military draft actually operates in ways many Congressmen, even a large majority, did not intend. The difference between the intention and the real world is in large part a result of the way the Supreme Court has stretched the meaning of the draft law's words because it was sensitive to First Amendment claims of religious freedom. That is why an objector case is included here.[25]

In both the Civil War and World War I the draft law was purposely designed to allow conscientious objection only to members of those religious groups known to teach pacifism as a part of their faith—that is, the historic "peace churches" like the Amish, the Quakers, and the Adventists. This was problematic for two reasons: first, a few members of other denominations claimed that their faith required conscientious objector classification; second, if members of these religious groups were given special treatment, was it not a kind of establishment of religion forbidden by the First Amendment?

Confronted with these problems, the Selective Service Administration in World War I interpreted the law so that it covered all who "by reason of religious training and belief" were opposed to war. Congress let this broadened interpretation stand by inaction, for its leaders certainly knew of the modification by interpretation.

Indeed, in 1940 Congress rephrased the law to include exactly what the administrators had developed as a makeshift. It exempted those who "by reason of religious training and belief" opposed participation in war. But it wanted "religious" to mean religious, and, therefore, it expressly denied exemption to those who opposed war on political, philosophical, sociological, or personal moral grounds.

But some courts continued interpreting clear words contrary to their meaning. A court of appeals decided that religion could include the promptings of some "inward mentor." Most people, including congressmen, would never classify such promptings as religious. This made for confusion, as another court of appeals went the straight and narrow way, insisting that when Congress said religious belief it did not mean some personal moral code unique to its holder. Notice, since the Supreme Court did not act on this matter for years, the law of the land was applied differently in two judicial circuits. Equal justice under law is hard to realize in the real world.

In 1948 and later, Congress reaffirmed its demand that religious objectors alone could be exempted from the draft. Section 6(j) of the Universal Military Training and Service Act used some of the same words as those used in 1940, adding these others to help clarify matters. "Religious training and belief means an individual's belief in relation to a Supreme Being involving duties superior to those arising from any human relation, but does not include essentially political, sociological, or philosophical views or a merely personal moral code."

Alas for simplicity, there were the same problems still. Some Eastern religions do not include belief in a Supreme Being. Does this phrase then unconstitutionally discriminate against their adherents in violation of due process of law? And closely related to that issue, does this law not give a special preference to religious people and their beliefs? Is that not an establishment of religion? Many people thought the law was fatally defective. What did the courts decide?

United States v. *Seeger*, 1965, showed the Supreme Court's inclination.[26] Daniel A. Seeger said on his conscientious objector form that he could not say he believed in the existence of God. However, he believed in "goodness and virtue for their own sakes" and had a "religious faith in a purely ethical creed." Could that qualify under the words of Congress?

The Supreme Court held that it could. By using the term "Supreme Being," Justice Clark said, Congress implied something broader than a personal deity familiar in Judeo-Christian orthodoxy. The test was this: did the belief constitute, "A sincere and meaningful belief which occupies in the life of the possessor a place paralleled to that filled by the God of those admittedly qualifying for the exemption."

If the Court had not been so liberal in its interpretation of Congress' intent, consider what it would have been forced to explore. Lawyers for Seeger were arguing that if "religion" applied only to those who held a more or less traditional view of what "religion" and "Supreme Being" were, the whole law would have to be declared unconstitutional as an establishment of religion.

But could the words of Congress be applied to an agnostic or an out-and-out atheist? Could the Court stretch Congress' intent so far? Yes, it could, given the decision in *Welsh* v. *United States*.[27]

Elliot A. Welsh had crossed out the word *religious* in his application for objector status. He could only claim "training and belief" derived "by readings in . . . history and sociology." Was he eligible in spite of the words Congress used?

Yes, said Justice Black in a five to three decision. While not religious in a normal sense, Welsh's belief that the taking of life was wrong was held with a deep fervor that made it religious in the sense of the Seeger decision. Justice Harlan wrote a concurring opinion saying that the Supreme Court by this decision was repairing the shoddy work of Congress. Justices Burger, White, and Stewart dissented, arguing that congressional terms could not be stretched infinitely.

If the reader finds all of this difficult to understand in light of the notion that Congress makes policy and the courts apply that policy to specific cases, please remember the times. To hold against Welsh would have raised the question of the improper establishment of some religious beliefs that was mentioned earlier. Were that question raised, the Court might have had to strike down the conscientious objection section of the draft law. In 1970 there was already a great deal of trouble over the draft. If the Court had made the exempt status null and void, could Congress have acted at all or quickly enough to avoid sending thousands to jail? Who wanted to add such a controversial prospect to the fuels burning at the time? Judges read the newspapers too. Some of them are more wedded to the national welfare than to a strict construction of problematic laws.

Other Decisions Supporting Freedom

Besides these decisions, the Supreme Court has upheld the claim of the free exercise of religion against local officials enforcing ordinances which: prohibited the distribution of circulars on the streets without a permit; [28] forbade handbill distribution without a license under an antilittering rule; [29] made it a felony, no less, to preach or teach in a way that discouraged the saluting of the flag; [30] prohibited the circulation of handbills that advertised religious books and asked for donations for religious purposes; [31] excluded a religious canvasser from a company-owned town; [32] gave an unguided discretion to officials to forbid public preaching aided by a loudspeaker system; [33] and discriminated against one religious sect in the use of a public park.[34] Further, in 1978 the Court struck down a Tennessee state law which prohibited ministers from running for office. In part, the justices grounded their opinions in this case on the free exercise clause.[35]

Not all of these cases were settled squarely on the grounds of religious freedom. Freedom of speech, press, and assembly were also at issue. So too was a rather general "freedom of expression." But all of them began because a person in the name of religious belief had something to express to a world that included some folk who did not like to hear it.

Notes

[1] It is not always possible to say that a specific decision did or did not turn on freedom of religion. A case may arise from a religious liberty claim and finally be settled on grounds of free speech, free assembly, free press, or the religious establishment clause. Thus, totals in these matters must be rough as must be judgments concerning which case can or cannot be included in chapters like this.

[2] Kunz v. New York, 340 U.S. 290 (1951).

[3] Martin v. City of Struthers, 319 U.S. 141 (1943).

[4] Jones v. Opelika, 316 U.S. 584 (1942); Murdock v. Pennsylvania, 319 U.S. 105 (1943). Since Murdock came so close to the Jones decision and since the two cases were identical, the Court ordered a rehearing of Jones v. Opelika

when it heard *Murdock*. Thus, in 1943, the second Jones v. Opelika, 319 U.S. 103, was announced. In harmony with *Murdock*, it overturned the 1942 *Jones* decision.

[5] For a thorough overview of Jehovah's Witnesses cases and an assessment of Covington's record, see David R. Manwaring, *Render Unto Caesar* (Chicago: University of Chicago Press, 1962).

[6] Follett v. Town of McCormick, 321 U.S. 573 (1944).

[7] West Virginia State Board of Education v. Barnette, 319 U.S. 624 (1943).

[8] Minersville School District v. Gobitis, 310 U.S. 586 (1940).

[9] Jones v. Opelika, 316 U.S. 584 (1942).

[10] All of this and a meticulous analysis of the flag salute case is carefully documented in Manwaring.

[11] Wooley v. Maynard, 430 U.S. 705 (1977).

[12] Pierce v. Society of Sisters, 268 U.S. 510 (1925).

[13] See Walfred H. Peterson, "Some State Controls on Influences on Church Related Education" *Religion Education*, Vol. XLIII, No. 1. January–February, 1968, pp. 42–52.

[14] Wisconsin v. Yoder, 406 U.S. 205 (1972).

[15] Walter Berns, "Ratiocinations: The Importance of Being Amish," *Harpers*, March, 1973, pp. 33 ff.

[16] Sherbert v. Verner, 374 U.S. 398 (1963).

[17] The Sunday Law Cases, 366 U.S. 420, 582, 599, 617 (1961).

[18] Presbyterian Church in the United States v. Mary Elizabeth Blue Hull Memorial Presbyterian Church, 393 U.S. 440 (1969). In 1976 the Supreme Court used the same principles to settle the case of The Serbian Eastern Orthodox Diocese . . . v. Milivojevich, 426 U.S. 696.

[19] A description of his history is found in Mark DeWolfe Howe, *The Garden and the Wilderness* (Chicago: University of Chicago Press, 1965), pp. 32–60.

[20] Watson v. Jones, 13 Wall 679 (1872).

[21] For a brief but thorough study of these developments that omits religious rights, seek David P. Flint, "Justice Through Delegation: 1929–1970," *The Prison Journal*, Vol. LI, No. 2, Autumn-Winter, 1971, pp. 15–36.

[22] See David P. Flint, "Problems of Providing Justice for the Imprisoned" (Consumers of Justice Workshop Paper, American Political Science Association Meeting, 1971), pp. 8–12.

[23] Cruz v. Beto, 405 U.S. 319 (1972).

[24] See the concurring opinion of Judge Lowenthal in Anderson v. Laird, 466 Fed. R. 2nd., pp. 297–305.

[25] Two rather complete yet different surveys of the history of the law of the conscientious objector are available in Richard E. Morgan, *The Supreme Court and Religion* (New York: The Free Press, 1972), pp. 164–182 and Leo Pfeffer,

God, Caesar and the Constituion (Boston: Beacon Press, 1975), pp. 150–157.

[26] United States v. Seeger, 380 U.S. 163 (1965).

[27] Welsh v. United States, 398 U.S. 333 (1970).

[28] Lovell v. Griffin, 303 U.S. 444 (1938).

[29] Schneider v. Irvington, 308 U.S. 147 (1939).

[30] Taylor v. Mississippi, 319 U.S. 583 (1943).

[31] Jamison v. Texas, 318 U.S. 413 (1943).

[32] Marsh v. Alabama, 326 U.S. 501 (1946).

[33] Saia v. New York, 334 U.S. 558 (1948).

[34] Niemotko v. Maryland, 340 U.S. 268 (1951) and Fowler v. Rhode Island, 345 U.S. 67 (1953).

[35] McDaniel v. Paty, 55 LEd 2d, 593 (1978).

5
Decisions Against a Claim of Religious Liberty

Introduction

The previous chapter may have made it seem that religious liberty cases are easily won before the Supreme Court. Not so. Many have been lost. We now turn to several of the most important of these.

Here, as earlier, the reader will notice that usually, though not always, members of smaller religious groups appear as the initiators of the cases—Jehovah's Witnesses, Jews, Seventh-Day Adventists, Mormons. There is reason for this. Minority groups and their members are likely to be ignored or slighted in the democratic lawmaking process. There is no need to attribute hostile intent to our representatives for this, though, as the Jehovah's Witness cases show, such intent is not unheard of. Rather, in the busy, workaday world of legislators and administrators, who are themselves commonly members of the larger religious denominations, the peculiar needs of the lesser-known groups or of "odd" individuals simply get shunted aside.

This is one reason for the Bill of Rights. The larger groups and their members can generally make their needs and demands known to government with some success. But minorities must have their rights spelled out in black-and-white as a constant warning sign, lest the tyranny of the elected majority, perhaps absentmindedly, comes into play.

Nevertheless, no one from whatever group or from no group ought to imagine that religious freedom is absolute because a Bill of Rights declares that it exists. Governments have power to limit and to define. Society has need of some uniformity, as the following cases show.

Government Can Define Morality

In the United States the "police powers" are reserved to the fifty states by the Constitution. These broad powers, lawyers say, are those necessary to promote health, welfare, safety, and morals. Therefore, most conflicts between people claiming that their action is a product of their religion and a government claiming that the action violates some moral precept written into law involves a state government. But when such a dispute arises in Washington, D.C. or in the territories of the United States, then the federal government gets involved. So it was in *Reynolds* v. *United States* which developed in the territory of Utah, reaching the Supreme Court in 1878.[1]

George Reynolds was a Mormon who practiced bigamy. Residing in federal territory, he was charged with, and convicted of, violating federal law.

Reynold's defense was grounded squarely on religious freedom. He showed the Court that he was a member of the Church of Jesus Christ of Latter-Day Saints and that his church's doctrine made it the "duty of male members . . . , circumstances permitting, to practice polygamy." The duty, said the appellant, rested on teachings of holy books, including the Bible, and on a divine revelation to Joseph Smith, the church's founder. Further, his church had given Reynolds permission to enter a polygamous marriage, and one of its officials had performed the marriage ceremony which caused his arrest.

Since these facts were clear enough, the Supreme Court could put the question that was before it succinctly: Can religious beliefs be accepted as a justification of an overt act made criminal by the law of the land? The Court found it easy to arrive at the answer, resting on statements of Madison and Jefferson which distinguished between opinions and action. The free exercise clause made the former untouchable by law. The latter, however, could be controlled. "Congress was deprived (by the First Amendment) of all legislative power over mere opinion, but was left free to reach actions which were in violation of social duties or subversive of good order."

After saying that, the opinion of Chief Justice Waite explored the history of English and American laws against polygamy, showing that all the states, including those with constitutional protections of freedom of religion, had laws against it. These were not legislated without reason. Good social order required it. The chief justice cited an early social scientist and a British jurist to prove that a healthy democracy and society required the monogamous family. Since it did, Congress was within its legislative power when it proscribed polygamy.

But should the law be enforced against those whose religious beliefs require plural marriage? Yes. "To permit this (practice) would be to make the professed doctrines of religious belief superior to the law of the land, and in effect to permit every citizen to become a law unto himself. Government could exist only in name under such circumstances."

Until just a few years ago this seemed like a quaint case. Times change. Today, state laws respecting marriage practices are under attack on a variety of grounds. It would not be surprising if a similar case arose again.

If such a case came to the court tomorrow and if the justices agreed to accept it, the opinion might well be different even if the outcome were the same. The "belief-yes-action-no rule" [2] of the Reynolds case might not be followed. After all, the First Amendment protects the free *exercise* of religion. Does that not imply action?

Government Can Promote Health

Many religious groups have held beliefs about what was and was not a proper way to promote good health. These beliefs have often been regarded as central to the faith—so central that actions contrary to them were grievous sin. As governments became more and more active in promoting health by law, it was inevitable that their requirements would offend the beliefs of some of these groups deeply. Then, some of their members would not comply, regardless of consequences.

The United States Supreme Court has never decided a case squarely on such a conflict. But it did so, in effect, when it wrote its opinion in *Jacobson* v. *Massachusetts* in 1905.[3]

Henning Jacobson refused to be vaccinated for smallpox, though Cambridge, Massachusetts, required it by an ordinance. After arrest, trial, and conviction, he appealed to the state supreme court. He lost. Then, to the United States Supreme Court he went on grounds that forced vaccination violated the Preamble of the Constitution, the spirit of the Constitution, and rights secured by the Fourteenth Amendment, especially the right against having privileges and immunities abridged and against being deprived of liberty without due process of law.

To any competent lawyer it should have been clear that Jacobson was grasping mostly at straws. The Preamble, then as now, has never been a source of legal rights. Also, the Court could quote authoritatively from Chief Justice John Marshall concerning the legal use of the spirit of the Constitution "(T)he spirit is to be collected chiefly from its words." Two of Jacobson's pleas briefly dispatched, Justice Harlan for a unanimous Court went to the Fourteenth Amendment. Did its clauses protect Jacobson?

No. Massachusetts through the local ordinance was exercising its police power to protect the state's health. Such powers may invade the liberties of individuals in some cases. "But the liberty secured by the Constitution . . . does not import an absolute right in each person to be, at all times and in all circumstances, wholly free from restraint." Why not? "Upon the principle of self-defense, of paramount necessity, a community has the right to protect itself against an epidemic." Put more bluntly, for some purposes the good of the whole is more important than the freedom of the part.

How does this relate to Cambridge's vaccination ordinance? Smallpox is a dangerous, communicable disease. Vaccination protects against its spread. A law requiring vaccination is a reasonable exercise of state police power even though it offends the liberty of some.

In saying this the Court added a phrase of interest to us. It said that for "self-defense" and "paramount necessity" a state could compel a person to act contrary to "even his religious . . . conviction." Thus, though Jacobson had not argued on the basis of religious freedom, this case became a leading case respecting religious rights. Later Supeme Court decisions on the free exercise clause quoted this opinion. State courts also cited these words in cases argued on religious grounds, using them as they upheld state health measures, both as these affected adults and children.

It must be noted, however, that some state courts for purposes *touching only one person's health* have upheld a claim of religious liberty to refuse medical aid. Thus, in some states a Jehovah's Witness can refuse to have a blood transfusion. A Witness cannot, however, refuse to have a transfusion performed for a minor in his custody. A doctor can get a court order requiring that a transfusion be given to a child. This means that for legal purposes, the state's interest in a child may override the interest of the parents.[4]

All this is to say that in spite of some rather literal readings of the Bill of Rights, no person lives unto himself alone. If an action or inaction hurts someone else, the state may regulate it. The courts will say the regulation must be "reasonable." Reasonable to whom? Reasonable to them, of course.

Government Can Keep Order

Not only can freedom be limited by a government bent upon promoting some sort of moral precept or health practice but also it can be limited in the name of public order. So said a unanimous Court in *Cox* v. *New Hampshire* in 1941.[5]

Manchester, New Hampshire, had an ordinance requiring people who paraded on "public streets and ways" to obtain a parade permit. A small fee was charged for the permit, the amount being set to cover administrative costs and possible special costs the city incurred in policing the parade.

Cox and eighty-seven other Jehovah's Witnesses paraded with signs on the sidewalks and across streets in single file in several groups of about fifteen or twenty each. They did so on a Saturday night in the crowded business district, where, city officials said, as many as 26,000 people passed a single corner in an hour going about their business.

The Witnesses had obtained no parade permit. Sixty-eight were arrested, charged, and convicted of violating the law. They lost appeals in New Hampshire. So, they moved on to the federal Supreme Court where they were defended by Hayden C. Covington.

Claiming that a religious parade was worship, their attorney rested his argument largely on the free exercise clause. He also argued that the ordinance was unconstitutionally vague.

The Supreme Court handled the charge of vagueness by noting that as interpreted by the New Hampshire Supreme Court, there was nothing vague about the law. Indeed, it was rather precisely focused on groups parading in an organized way.

More important in the opinion was the discussion of the Witnesses' general "civil liberties" to express their religious beliefs. (The Court refused to call a parade "worship.") Here Justice Hughes had little trouble. He found that the permit requirement was a reasonable effort "to conserve public convenience." It gave the city notice of when and where a parade would occur. Police could then better provide for handling any problems of congestion it might create. The Witnesses had not shown that the permits were issued in a discriminatory way or that the small fee charged was unreasonable.

Thus, the Court said, no civil liberty was denied. The permit requirement did not deny the acknowledged right to hand out literature or inform people of beliefs. And the permit did not give any official the power to determine what was and what was not religious as had been the problem in the earlier case of *Cantwell* v. *Connecticut.* The Witnesses had no legitimate grievance.

Since this decision rested on the need for public order in 1941, we must assume it is still valid today. The Supreme Court sits just across from the Capitol near Pennsylvania Avenue. It cannot help but feel that the regulation of traffic is a necessity in the age of crowds and of the internal combustion engine. Indeed, in retrospect, the argument of the Witnesses seems petty. Their history in this period might be read to indicate that they preferred confrontation with the police as a means of getting attention and, perhaps, of proving something to themselves. Where freedom exists it may be used for ulterior purposes by anyone.

Government Can Promote Child Welfare

As with morality, health, and order, so, too, with welfare. Government can promote it over some religious liberty claims. But there is welfare and welfare, and a state's concern for child welfare is more easily justified than is its concern for adult welfare when a conflicting demand for freedom is at stake. This we learn from *Prince* v. *Massachusetts,* 1943.[6]

Sarah Prince was a Jehovah's Witness and the aunt and guardian of Betty Simmons. Betty, a nine-year-old, was given religious magazines and permitted to offer them for sale by her guardian. Both furnishing of articles for sale to children and permitting a child under twelve years of age to sell them violated Massachusetts' child labor laws. Sarah Prince was arrested, tried, and convicted under these laws. Losing in Massachusetts' courts, she turned to the federal Supreme Court. Again, Hayden C. Covington argued the Witness' case.

Perhaps better understanding can be had if the following facts are known. Betty testified that she also was a Witness who wanted to "preach" and "worship" through the sale of magazines. Indeed, the record showed that she and Mrs. Prince's two young sons tearfully pleaded with Sarah Prince for the privilege of public selling on the night of the offense.

The arresting officer was a truant officer, who found Betty on the street near her guardian at around 8:30 P.M. on a December night. He had warned Mrs. Prince previously that any such "work" by children violated the law.

Justice Rutledge, finding in favor of the state, wrote the majority opinion. It did not satisfy four of his brethren. Three concurred with the decision for reasons which Justice Jackson presented. Justice Murphy dissented alone vigorously. Thus, compared to the Reynolds, Jacobson, and Cox cases, the Court here found the issues more difficult.

Rutledge began with a major concession. First Amendment freedoms, he said, have a "preferred position." That is, they must be awarded the highest priority in any ordering of constitutional rights and powers. Since the Constitution itself makes no such demand, this was a significant judicial interpretation of our fundamental law.

But even a "preferred" right, the justice concluded, could be overridden for the sake of the welfare of children. They needed special protection, especially when labor in public places was the concern. Children had rights and families had rights to direct children, but the state's power to promote child welfare could limit those rights.

In concurring, Justice Jackson argued that selling magazines to the random public on the streets was really a secular act that the state could control. It was not like passing the plate in a voluntarily assembled religious congregation. It was more like a church's public bingo game. Being secular, the selling unquestionably could be regulated.

Justice Murphy dissented. To him the burden of proof was on the state. Why? Because, as the majority said, First Amendment freedoms were in a "preferred position." Did the state show that it had a compelling interest in the welfare of Betty Simmons given the facts on the record? No. There simply was no proof of any "grave and immediate" danger to the child. Such proof was required when the government restricted religious liberty.

Then the justice closed with a powerful plea:

No chapter in human history has been so largely written in terms of persecution and intolerance as the one dealing with religious freedom. From ancient times to the present day, the ingenuity of man has known no limits in his ability to forge weapons of oppression for use against those who dare to express or practice unorthodox religious beliefs. And the Jehovah's Witnesses are living proof of the fact that even in this nation, conceived as it was in the ideals of freedom, the right to practice religion in unconventional ways is still far from secure. Theirs is a militant and unpopular faith, pursued with a fanatic's zeal. They have suffered brutal beatings, their property has been destroyed; they have been harassed at every turn by the resurrection and enforcement of little used ordinances and statutes. To them, along with other present-day religious minorities, befalls the burden of testing our devotion to the ideals and constitutional guarantees of religious freedom. We should therefore hesitate before approving the application of a statute that might be used as another instrument of oppression. Religious freedom is too sacred a right to be restricted or prohibited in any degree without convincing proof that a legitimate interest of the state is in grave danger.

Remarkably, that magnificent plea did not bring Justices Douglas or Black to Murphy's side, in spite of their reputations as champions of freedom.

Government Can Promote Welfare for All

The Court's difficulty in the Prince case was not great compared to what it experienced in four Sunday law cases decided in 1961.[7] In these its several opinions took up well over 200 pages of the *Supreme Court Reports,* even though the different cases raised the same constitutional issues in the minds of those who started them on their way up the judicial ladder.

Two of the four need not concern us here, since they were not treated as properly raising free exercise issues. They will be discussed below together with cases centered on the meaning of the establishment of religion clause.

Two, however, were settled on grounds of freedom of reli-

gion, if *settled* is the right word. There was no majority opinion
for these. Chief Justice Warren wrote an opinion that Justices
Black, Clark, and Whittaker could sign. Justice Frankfurter concurred with an opinion that Justice Harlan found acceptable. Douglas, Brennan, and Stewart each needed a separate
opinion for their dissents.

Involved in these cases were state laws which required
that most businesses be closed on Sunday. Anyone familiar with
such laws knows immediately what they are like. They begin
by forbidding the operation of all or almost all businesses on
Sunday. Then they add a long list of exceptions. Some of the
exceptions seem rather reasonable as, for example, those which
permit the sale of medicine and gasoline. But many of the
exceptions seem rather silly as, for example, some found in a
New York law still operating into the 1960s which permitted
the sale of bread, cake, milk, and eggs any time on Sunday,
but prohibited the sale of butter and cheese after 10 A.M.,
except in delicatessen stores between 4 and 7:30 P.M.[8]

Obviously, such laws can and do work a hardship on Sabba-
tarains, principally, but not only, Orthodox Jews and Seventh-
Day Adventists. As employees and employers, the impact of
Sunday closing legislation is to limit them to a five-day week—
indeed, to less than that for the Orthodox Jews who begin
their sabbath observance at sundown on Friday.

As a result of this hardship, Sabbatarians have argued repeatedly before the courts that Sunday closing laws violate
their freedom of religion. But in this claim they have been
unsuccessful. Chief Justice Warren tried to explain why in what
must be called the most authoritative legal statement on the
subject, even if he could not get a majority to accept his assumptions and logic.

The chief justice conceded that Sabbatarians were "bur-
dened economically" by the total impact of their beliefs and
the two states' day of rest requirements. But the burden was
only *indirectly* due to the law. The law penalized no belief
at all. It was an exercise of the states' welfare powers affecting

only actions. This power for secular, not religious, reasons was used to give people a weekly period of rest, quiet, and family togetherness. "To strike down . . . legislation which imposes only an indirect burden on the exericse of religion, i.e., legislation which does not make unlawful the religious practice itself, would radically restrict the operating latitude of the legislature."

But should the states use an alternative means of providing a day of rest which would not create this burden? Should the Court force them to grant an exemption for Sabbatarians which would require only that a business be closed either Saturday or Sunday? The chief justice again said no. While such an alter native might be wise, it was not a constitutional requirement. It was not arbitrary or unreasonable to suppose that a single rest day promoted the whole society's welfare better than the suggested alternative. Also, permitting businesses to choose which day they would close on the basis of belief, might produce unfair economic competition. It might make the state inquire into the sincerity of a business person's belief if the person chose to be open on Sunday. In short, the suggested alternative might be less effective in meeting the state's objective, very problematic for businesses in general, and difficult to enforce.

The three dissenters argued that such laws needlessly limited people's religious freedom. The alternatives available were constitutionally required. Justice Douglas made, perhaps, the most telling point. What if the law had specified Saturday as the single day of rest? Would not Sunday observers feel their rights were denied?

Government Controls Draft Exemption

Recall from chapter 4 that while the free exercise clause of the First Amendment stands in the close background of conscientious objectors cases, the Supreme Court has held repeatedly that a person can be exempted from the draft on religious grounds solely on the basis of Congress' grace. That is, there is *no constitutional right* to exempt status. That status is a matter of transient law, not of the enduring Bill of Rights.

The Supreme Court, as we also learned in chapter 4, was willing to stretch the law of Congress so far as to make an agnostic or atheist eligible for objector classification. This took a lot of stretching because Congress had purposely defined the religious reason for objection in a rather traditional way to exclude people not somehow inspired by Judeo-Christian beliefs.

In 1971 a nation deeply troubled by the Vietnam War found that there were limits to the judicial stretching of some terms. The Supreme Court had been asked if a conscientious objector to *only* the Vietnam War was eligible for the draft law's exemption. In the past both Congress and the courts had recognized as grounds for objector classification beliefs that involved opposition to *all* wars. Could the Supreme Court, capable of stretching "religious" as traditionally defined to cover atheists, stretch Congress' law to cover those who found just one war, like the war in Vietnam, immoral?

In spite of one earlier Court opinion that did a bit of stretching in this direction,[9] and in spite of a district court opinion that said it must be done,[10] the Supreme Court refused to be flexible on the matter of "selective objection." In *Gillette* v. *United States* it handed down a decision which closely followed Congress' intent.[11] Congress clearly meant, Justice Thurgood Marshall said, for the majority, to grant conscientious objector exemption to those who opposed *war*, not just this or that war. This limited grant, he said, had wisdom in it, for a draft board would find it most difficult to judge the sincerity of an objection to a single war. Therefore, the fairness of the draft system would be called into question if such objections were considered.

Then Marshall took up the issue which had been in the background of many earlier objector cases. Does the grant of exemption to some on the basis of their "religious" beliefs give them a legal preference? Isn't this an unconstitutional establishment of religion?

No establishment of religion is created in this case, said the majority. As interpreted in Seeger and Welsh, the exemption is not religious in a way that runs afoul the antiestablishment clause. It has become importantly secular in quality. Further, the single, all-war exemption requires less government entanglement with religion than would an exemption that permitted argument on the morality of each and every war. The antiestablishment clause was designed to minimize church-state entanglement. Congress' law did that.

Justice Douglas dissented for himself alone. He wanted to get to fundamentals. Conscientious objectors should not have to base their exemption from the draft on a law passed by Congress. They should have exemption as a First Amendment right. That Amendment protected persons from laws that offended their religion or conscience. In this case, Gillette's "selective objection" to the war in Vietnam was his constitutionally protected right. The Court erred in permitting that such as he be drafted. The justice found not a single supporter on the bench.

The conclusions are several. The Court will stretch terms it will and will not stretch terms it will not. Predictions are hazardous. While the First Amendment may influence the Court in its stretching of the word *religious,* the law of Congress, not that Amendment, is still all the conscientious objector can rest on. The grant of exemption to some for "religious" reasons is not an establishment of religion.

Government Controls Tax Classification

Few, if any, would raise their eyebrows on being told that government controls tax classification. Of course, it must. Government's life blood is taxes. It has to create a tax system and enforce it by its own definitions. How does this relate to religious freedom?

Tax classification affects religious freedom because a religious organization may grow and prosper under preferred or tax-exempt status. Then, its status may be changed by the government to the organization's great disadvantage. The following case illustrates this point, even though the Supreme Court refused to hear it on appeal. Thus, we must rely here for the first time on a United States Court of Appeals opinion. There is nothing wrong with that reliance, of course, for it too is the law of the land. But the ring of its authority is not quite so clear as that of a Supreme Court opinion.

Christian Echoes National Ministry, Inc. v. *United States* was decided by the three-judge Tenth Circuit Court of Appeals in Denver in 1972.[12] It overturned a district court ruling concerning the proper tax classification for Christian Echoes, a corporation presided over by the nationally known evangelist and anticommunist, Dr. Billy James Hargis, of Tulsa, Oklahoma.

The corporation had been created "to establish and maintain weekly religious radio and television broadcasts, . . . a national religious magazine and other religious publications, (and) . . . religious educational institutions." Its statement of faith included one paragraph which centered attention on "atheistic world forces" that were trying to destroy all religions, especially Christianity, and all free governments.

In 1953 the Internal Revenue Service (IRS) ruled that Christian Echoes should be classified as a tax-exempt religious and educational organization under Section 501(c)(3) of the tax law. That section gives exemption to "religious, charitable, scientific, (research) . . . , literary or educational" nonprofit organizations. However, it specifically does not include agencies whose activities in "substantial part" attempt to influence legislation or those who promote "any political campaign on behalf of any candidate for public office."

Billy James Hargis' preaching and publications were consistently a mixture of revivalist religion and vigorous anticommunism. His pronouncements also related to domestic politics, supporting conservative and far-right causes. The IRS somehow noted this and starting in 1962 reviewed the corporation's tax classification. In 1964 Christian Echoes was told its exemption was revoked. This action not only required that it pay taxes but also meant that contributions to it were not tax-deductible for individuals.

Christian Echoes protested the decision and was told that its activities were in such large measure political that it did not belong under the exempt class.

The corporation went to federal district court. There Judge Allen E. Barrow decided in its favor. The judge found that Hargis' motives were religious. More important for our purposes, he ruled that "the First Amendment prohibits the Government . . . from determining whether the (contested) activities are religious or political." Further, Judge Barrow said that "due process of law" had been violated, because Christian Echoes had been "arbitrarily selected" out from many other similar organizations for reevaluation of its tax status.

In a series of complicated legal maneuvers, the case reached the court of appeals which reversed Judge Barrow's decision. What were the grounds?

Writing for the appellate court, Circuit Judge James E. Barrett, found that Christian Echoes was deeply involved in politics and partisan political causes.

The corporation's magazine, *Christian Crusade*, pushed all sorts of political endeavors—twenty-two were listed by the judge. These included writing letters to congressmen, working in party precincts, supporting numerous bills and constitutional amendments, opposing the national news media, demanding American withdrawal from the United Nations, and withdrawal of recognition of the USSR. To the court of appeals all this activity in combination, at least, was called "political activity" under IRS regulations.

The aim of IRS efforts in this regard was to be neutral in political matters. This required that it not give an indirect subsidy to organizations through tax exemption. Since the political work of the Hargis organization was "substantial and continuous," tax exemption constituted the sort of subsidy that Congress meant to deny for such activity when it drafted the Internal Revenue Code.

But is this not a limit on freedom of religion? No, said the court. Tax exemption is a privilege given by Congress, not a right. That is, *exemption stems from the law not from the First Amendment.* Further, Christian Echoes was still free to broadcast and publish as it saw fit. If that activity continued to be substantially political, it would have to pay the price for being political. If that activity became substantially less political, its tax status would be reviewed and exemption again granted.

What of the contention that Christian Echoes had been especially singled out for review? The district judge had agreed that it had been and that such discriminatory treatment violated the Fifth Amendment's due process clause. The court of appeals disagreed. It found the tax review was reasonably related to known facts of Christian Echoes' operations.

When the case was appealed to the Supreme Court, Billy James Hargis found himself among some friends of temporary convenience. At his side with an amicus curiae brief was the National Council of Churches, an organization which Hargis often attacked with strong words. There also stood the Baptist Joint Committee on Public Affairs and the American Baptist Convention, neither honored by Christian Echoes. Why did these come to the aid of their longtime critic?

These organizations supported Hargis because they were keenly interested in IRS rules which distinguish between *religious* and *political.* They all did much lobbying and were proud of it. Looking at Hargis' problems they could well say, "There but for the grace of the IRS go I."

With only Justice Douglas objecting, the Supreme Court refused to hear the case.[13] Therefore, the court of appeals decision became final. Christian Echoes lost its exemption. Hargis said on hearing of the Supreme Court's inaction, "This is a sad day for all religion. Freedom of speech and . . . worship . . . ended today." Dean Kelley of the National Council of Churches reacted with a different fear. To him the case meant that the IRS had a "blank check to harass religious groups with unpopular views."

Kelley's warning may have been prophetic for some groups. In 1974 a unanimous Supreme Court upheld an IRS decision which revoked tax exemption for Bob Jones University, because it refused to admit black students [14] on the basis, it said, of religious principles. And on the same day a seven-to-one Court upheld the revocation of exemption for the Washington, D.C. educational and lobbying agency, Americans United for Separation of Church and State.[15] Like Bob Jones University, Americans United raised First Amendment issues which the Court found were not yet ripe for settlement.

Whatever the merits of the law and of the IRS action on these cases, anyone who lived through the Watergate episode may wonder if the IRS decided to "pick on" these two organizations and on Christian Echoes as a means of punishing them for their political views and of warning other organizations that Big Brother is watching. To suppress that unpleasant thought is to be unrealistic about how politics is sometimes—only sometimes—conducted.

Other Decisions Against a Claim of Freedom

The United States Supreme Court has handed down other decisions which denied a claim of the free exercise of religion. These included the following: allowing an Idaho law to stand which denied the vote to anyone who would not take an oath denying that he was a bigamist or a member of a probigamist association; [16] upholding a federal law annulling the charter of the Mormon Church and seizing its properties not used for worship because of the Mormon's promotion of illegal acts; [17] permitting the University of California to expel a student who on the basis of conscience refused to take an ROTC course; [18] affirming a New Hampshire conviction of a person arrested for swearing at an officer, though the words were claimed to be a religious expression; [19] and allowing the Illinois State Bar Association to deny membership and with it the right to practice law to a conscientious objector.[20]

Also noted above in the Walz case, the Court sometimes brushes aside a claim of religious freedom as it decides a case on other grounds.

A Concluding Note

Between this and previous chapters we have now covered eighteen cases in some detail and referred to others in which the Supreme Court drew a line between what was and what was not someone's religious liberty. This line-drawing process in response to real people with what they thought were real grievances is the most authoritative way in which the meaning of religious liberty is defined.

As the most authoritative means of definition, it is just the barest tip of the iceberg of all the religious liberty issues raised in our society. Far below the tip, thousands of lesser-known officials are making decisions. A school principal decides whether a religious group can use a schoolroom for some program. A city council decides whether a park can be the location of an outdoor evangelistic service. A county council passes an ordinance concerning door-to-door solicitation and advertising. A county judge issues an order to give a child some medical treatment, overriding the religious wishes of a parent. A state legislature enacts a statute on the observance of what some believe is a religious holiday. The Federal Communications Commission adopts a regulation that relates to religious broadcasts on radio and television. The examples are endless, and together they define fully the religious liberty in the society.

But no one can encompass all those actions. And since the Supreme Court applies "the supreme law of the land" most authoritatively, the officials who make this multitude of decisions tend to rely on its opinions, usually as interpreted to them by lawyers. So, the Supreme Court's definitions make up the most important definitions of religious liberty we have. Do these definitions give us a pattern of religious liberty? A formula we can rely on in case of dispute? A general "law of liberty?

Notes

1 Reynolds v. United States, 98 U.S. 145 (1878).

2 The phrase comes from Leo Pfeffer, *God, Caesar and the Constitution* (Boston: Beacon Press, 1975), pp. 31–36.

3 Jacobson v. Massachusetts, 197 U.S. 11 (1905).

4 For a fuller treatment of the blood transfusion and other related cases, see Leo Pfeffer, *Church, State and Freedom* (Boston: Beacon Press, 1967), pp. 696–706.

5 Cox v. New Hampshire, 312 U.S. 569 (1941).

6 Prince v. Massachusetts, 321 U.S. 158 (1943).

7 The two decided on free exercise grounds were Gallager v. Crown Kosher Super Market, 366 U.S. 617 (1961) and Braunfeld v. Brown, 366 U.S. 599 (1961). The two decided on establishment of religion were McGowan v. Maryland, 366 U.S. 420 (1961) and Two Guys from Harrison-Allentown v. McGinley, 366 U.S. 582 (1961). In 1977 the Supreme Court upheld under the Civil Rights Act of 1964, not the First Amendment, a private company's discharge of an employee whose refusal to work on Sunday upset the administration of seniority rules agreed upon by the company and a labor union: Trans World Airlines v. Haridson, 53 L. Ed. 2d. 113.

8 Leo Pfeffer has a collection of such odd exceptions in his *Church, State and Freedom*, pp. 273–278.

9 In 1955 the Supreme Court had allowed the exemption of a Jehovah's Witness who said he would fight in no "carnal" war. However, he would fight at the battle of Armageddon against Satan. Such a spiritual war didn't count in this world's affairs, said the Court in Sicurella v. United States, 348 U.S. 385.

10 United States v. Sisson, 297 F. Supp. 902 (D Mass. 1969).

11 Gillette v. United States, 401 U.S. 437 (1971).

12 Christian Echoes National Ministries, Inc. v. United States, 470 F. 2d 849 (1972). (In some books the names of the parties are reversed due to the complexity of appeals.)

13 United States v. Christian Echoes National Ministries, Inc., 404 U.S. 561 (1972), certiorari denied.

14 Bob Jones University v. Simon, 416 U.S. 725 (1974). In a related opinion rejecting the claim of free association, the Supreme Court said in 1976 that private schools could not discriminate on grounds of race: Runyon v. McCrary, 427 U.S. 160.

15 Alexander v. "Americans United," 416 U.S. 752 (1974).

16 Davis v. Beason, 133 U.S. 333 (1890).

17 Church of Jesus Christ of Latter-Day Saints v. United States, 136 U.S. I (1890).

18 Hamilton v. Regents of the University of California, 393 U.S. 245 (1934).

19 Chaplinsky v. New Hampshire, 315 U.S. 568 (1942).

20 In re Summers, 325 U.S. 561 (1945).

6

The Law of Religious Liberty: An Overview

Is There a *Law* of Religious Liberty?

In this chapter we begin with a question. Does the First Amendment provide us with a *law*—a general principle or general rule—which authoritatively defines religious freedom? The answer is a firm yes and no.

In very simple cases there is a general rule which clarifies the meaning of religious liberty. It comes straight from the First Amendment's words. There shall be no prohibition of the free exercise of religion.

Suppose, if you can, that on grounds of breach of the peace a policeman arrested the leaders of a quiet, peaceful, and very traditional worship service held in a private building because, the officer said, the religious ideas being voiced in the service might lead to riots at some uncertain, future time. Suppose, further, that a county attorney prosecuted the case. Competent judges from county courts to the Supreme Court would agree that for this case there was a clear law of religious liberty. The words "no prohibition" would satisfy to explicate it. The case would be settled as soon as the facts were known. Indeed, it would be thrown out of court, and the officer might well be sued for false arrest.

Obviously, this is not the sort of case that courts, especially appellate courts, hear. The cases they must decide are far more subtle and complex. Therefore, no simple law of religious liberty like the one just described is likely to be of much service.

For the more complex disputes, the Supreme Court has

been unable to arrive at a general rule or principle that clarifies how the First Amendment's free exercise clause is to be applied. Rather, in a groping, trial and error fashion it has used several principles for different cases, and, indeed, often the majority justices have disagreed on which general principle they, let alone the minority justices, were following. Therefore, it is impossible to formulate a single law of religious freedom for most real-life controversies that our higher courts must settle.

Supreme Court justices are not alone. Scholars who study the judges' opinions and criticize them for inconsistencies have not been agreed on any single law of religious freedom either. Philip Kurland of the University of Chicago School of Law in excoriating the Supreme Court for its failures on this score has developed a general principle he believes should be adopted.[1] Paul Kauper of the University of Michigan School of Law finds Kurland's effort historically and legally incorrect. Further, Kauper argues that Kurland's suggestion would be unwise.[2] C. Herman Pritchett of the University of Chicago's political science department agrees more with Kauper than with Kurland.[3] And the position of Leo Pfeffer on the subject is clearly different from that of Richard Morgan, both of whose works are frequently cited in these pages.[4]

All this means that a summary statement of the law of religious liberty must include a list of principles derived from the cases above. From this list judges may choose one principle or two or more principles and use them alone or in various combinations to help determine if the claim of freedom or the claim of state power is more compelling in a case.

Does this imply that the judges have room to allow their biases to work when they decide any but a rather simple case? Yes, yes, yes! Since several principles may be used by the judges, they have some freedom of judgment. *They are not required by the law to decide one certain way.* Therefore, a good lawyer arguing a religious liberty case before the Supreme Court, or any court, will study the law *and* the predispositions of the judges. We are in all but easy cases ruled by men *and* by laws. The unschooled may shout, "I know what my rights are!" Students of the law are not so sure.

The Laws of Religious Liberty

The Belief/Action Rule. Chief Justice Waite writing for a unanimous court in *Reynolds* v. *United States* stated one principle that merits attention only because it has been often repeated. "Congress was deprived of all legislative power over mere *opinion,* but was left free to reach *actions* which were in violation of social duties or subversive of good order." [5]

This statement is the basis for the assertion that under the Bill of Rights there is absolute freedom of belief. But when belief turns into action, then absolute freedom is no longer protected. Relative freedom comes to the fore.

Obviously, the belief/action rule has very little, if any, utility. Of course, belief is free if it is silent and completely internalized. The state will not even know about it!

Since belief becomes action as soon as a person moves or speaks or writes or creates a symbol to express that belief, all of the issues that concern us here are in the realm of action. And that is why the First Amendment protects not free belief but the free *exercise* of religion. Exercise is action.

Justice Waite's belief/action line, then, is best viewed as a sort of pregame, warm-up exercise often used by judges to get ready for the real contest. After verbalizing it in the opening paragraphs of an opinion, they move on to distinguish between proper and improper actions under the First Amendment. There the real struggles lie. There a rule is needed.

The Secular Regulation Rule. Developed in state courts in the nineteenth century, adopted in an unclear way by the Supreme Court in the Reynolds case, and still applied today in modified form for some purposes, the secular regulation rule is the longest lived of all efforts to show how the free exercise of religion can be meshed with the constitutional exercise of state power. The rule says that if the government regulates conduct by a statute within its power so as to promote a purely secular goal, the regulation is valid despite the fact that it may put a burden on or even forbid some religious practice.

In the Reynolds case the federal government's regulation against bigamy was a secular effort within federal power to protect against antisocial conduct in the territories. The fact that Mormons had their own religious mandate to the contrary could not overturn the regulation. In the Cox case New Hampshire's local ordinance requiring a parade permit was a secular demand within the state's power to maintain order. The fact that Jehovah's Witnesses believed they should not obtain a parade permit on religious grounds could not overturn the ordinance. In draft cases the Selective Service Acts were secular devices under the nation's defense powers to promote national security. The fact that some conscientious objectors had religious feelings to the contrary could not make the acts unconstitutional.

The utility of this rule is clear. It permits government to govern in a land which has many different religious groups practicing different ethical codes. If everyone's conscience could give an exemption to the law, the law might be unenforceable due to all the exemptions. Also, the thrust of the rule is to force governments to treat all religious groups and people alike, for in limiting governments to purely secular matters, it forbids that they dabble with exemptions to the law based on religious ideas. Put differently, the secular regulation rule, strictly followed, prohibits the preferential treatment of or the *establishment* of any religious belief.

The disutility of the rule is more obvious. It is very stingy with religious freedom. It would have forced children to salute the flag even though they believe the salute idolatrous. Why? Because education for patriotism is a secular function of the state. It made and still makes Sabbatarians close their business on Sunday even though they have already closed them for religious reasons on Saturday. Why? Because reserving a single day of rest each week is an exercise of secular welfare powers. The list of such illustrations could be endless in the twentieth century, for modern society assumes that almost all of life is secular.

By 1943 the majority Supreme Court had decided that the secular regulation rule, purely and simply applied, was too suppressive of freedom to be followed for some purposes. But the test was not flatly overruled. It appeared in later forms.

The Secular Regulation and Alternative Means Rule. The secular regulation rule was amended in two ways by judges who needed a more liberal standard given their predispostions. Justice Black's opinion in *Martin* v. *City of Struthers,* 1943, is a good illustration of one of these amendments. Remember that in that case the city had made it illegal to go door-to-door distributing circulars. Justice Black found this an unconstitutional restriction on religious expression.

The justice conceded that the city could limit door-to-door canvassing as a means to the promotion of a secular end— the quiet and convenience of its citizens. So far the secular regulation rule stood. But the flat prohibition of all canvassing was an excessively restrictive means to this reasonable end. There were *alternative means* to promote quiet and convenience that were less destructive of freedom. For example: The time of canvassing might be limited, or an ordinance could make it illegal to knock where the resident had posted a sign saying, "No Solicitors." Not *any* secular regulation was constitutional if there were available alternative means which better served liberty.

Chief Justice Warren's opinion in the Sunday law cases explored one proposed alternative means to blue laws. That means would have allowed Sabbatarians to close their businesses on Saturday instead of Sunday. The chief justice found that this alternative means would not satisfactorily achieve the desired state purposes of one single day of rest. Yet, the opinion used the alternative means idea in a serious way.

Certainly, this alternative means principle is likely to be

far more generous with freedom than the simple secular regulation rule. The Martin case shows the dimension of that generosity. Thus, the rule is espoused by many who try to maximize religious freedom. They make a valid point when they argue that this rule takes *both* government power and the Bill of Rights into account, unlike the old secular regulation rule which concentrated on power alone.

Criticism of the rule comes from judges and others who fear that, in effect, it makes the court assume legislative powers. In striking down a statute or ordinance under the rule, judges usually outline what the legislators might do instead. Thus, the separation of powers scheme in the federal and state constitutions is eroded by this rule's operation. Judges become lawmakers rather than law interpreters. Such lawmaking by judges is constitutionally improper and unwise. Judges do not hold hearings before they suggest such alternatives to the law. They do not listen to administrators and to the public, who have an idea of how the law might operate. Instead, on the basis of, perhaps, some brief comments by one or a few lawyers and on their own experience and theorizing, they boldly assert that some better alternative means could be used. Are they so informed as all that?

The Secular Regulation and the Direct/Indirect Effect Rule. The Sherbert case, described previously, yielded another variation on the secular regulation rule. Recall, in that case the Supreme Court said that Sherbert had a right to South Carolina's unemployment compensation even though she refused some jobs available to her that required Saturday work. Her refusal rested on the belief that Saturday was the sabbath.

One small part of Justice Brennan's decision took the position that if a secular regulation of the state had a *direct* impact on a person contrary to his conscience, it could not pass the requirement of the free exercise clause. If its effect on a person were only indirect, as with blue laws, then the secular regulation was acceptable.

As with the alternative means rule, the direct/indirect effect rule can be far more generous with liberty than the pure and simply secular regulation principle—a signal advantage. One disadvantage is obvious: What is the difference between a direct and indirect effect? Why was the impact of the loss of unemployment compensation on Sherbert said to be direct while the impact of a Sunday law on Braunfeld's business was labeled indirect? Another disadvantage is that if people's religious consciences exempt them from any law, does the exemption not give them special preference? Is preference for anyone's religion not forbidden by the establishment clause?

Whatever the pros and cons, by 1963 when the Sherbert decision was handed down, the old illiberal secular regulation rule had been heavily qualified. The Court would not kill it, but the Court's liberals on the free exercise clause had tamed it to suit their predispositions.

The Preferred Position Rule. The Supreme Court's liberals have tried other rules or principles to clarify why they stood ready to place religious freedom higher in the constitutional order of values than other considerations. Especially in the 1940s one or more of these justices was likely to announce, or come close to announcing, the preferred position principle. One version of this principle merely stated that in a face-to-face encounter, a First Amendment liberty must be preferred over the exercise of a government power. To quote Justice Murphy, concurring with Justices Douglas and Black in support of the majority in *Martin* v. *City of Struthers,* "Freedom of religion has a higher dignity under the Constitution than municipal and personal convenience." [6]

An even more sweeping statement of the preferred position is found in another opinion of Justice Murphy. In *Jones* v. *City of Opelika,* Murphy argued for himself and three other dissenters that free religion was superior even to free speech and press in our Constitutional scheme. "But there is another . . . reason why these ordinances cannot constitutionally apply to the petitioners. Important as free speech and a free press are to a free government and a free citizenry, there is a right even more dear to many individuals—the right to worship their Maker . . . and to carry their message to every living creature." [7]

The virtue of this position, besides its almost unbounded definition of freedom of religion, relates to an ancient, brute fact. Many devout religious folk will insist on expressing and acting out their beliefs in spite of "Caesar's" contrary orders. Thus, to avoid filling prisons with such people, let them say their piece and do their thing. When Justice Murphy was writing these words, Jehovah's Witnesses were just emerging from a period of persecution. Perhaps, he was trying to fashion a rule of the moment to get the nation past this sad and unnecessary episode. Of course, constitutional rules are not supposed to be rules of the moment.

One clear problem with this rule is that the Constitution itself gives no priority list. Government powers and the people's rights are found there, but no rank order appears. And certainly no rank order can be found in the First Amendment. So isn't the preferred position rule a rule found only in the minds of some justices? Yes. But what rule except the most obvious is not ultimately found there?

The Compelling Interest Rule. Something of a hybrid between the secular regulation rule and the preferred position standard is the compelling interest rule. Found in the majority opinion in both *Sherbert* v. *Verner,* 1963, and *Wisconsin* v. *Yoder,* 1972, this rule is what the Supreme Court is probably most likely to use in a religious liberty case today.

The reader may recollect that in the Yoder case the Court found a clear state interest in Wisconsin's compulsory school law—the education of the oncoming generation. It also found a clear claim of conscience—the Amish objection to the corrupting influences, in their view, of public secondary education. If courts could afford the luxury of being immobilized, such a balance of power and rights might have urged simple indecision.

Of course, the Supreme Court did decide—all but unanimously. Its formula was the compelling interest rule. As developed in Yoder, this rule is almost as complex as life itself. Here is an effort to distill its essence: Only where, in the light of pertinent factors, the state has a compelling interest in the enforcement of some law can that law be enforced in a way that overrides a claim of conscience.

In Yoder, the state of Wisconsin could easily argue it had a compelling interest in the education of the youth. Its brief said that both its economic and political well-being assumed a substantial education for its population. This argument would normally have carried the day. It failed to do so because the justices found a pertinent factor which made all the difference.

Because the Amish home and community educated the child very effectively in the simple arts their life-style required, the state's compelling interest disappeared. Justice Burger noted that Amish informal education actually seemed to be superior to public education in forming a young adult skilled in what her community required for its well-being.

Here is one advantage to the compelling interest test. As used in Yoder, it ensures that a wide range of pertinent factors will be considered before state power is upheld against a claim of conscience. This in turn yields another advantage. Since only a *compelling* interest qualified by all pertinent considerations has any constitutional advantage, the rule should usually be far more generous in protecting freedom than some others.

Further, the rule as developed by Justice Brennan in *Sherbert* v. *Verner* can be given a quantitative dimension. Few people, such as Sherbert, would be likely to ask for an exception to the state of South Carolina's unemployment compensation law. Thus, the state should have been more willing than it was to make an exception for Sabbatarians. It had no compelling interest where it denied benefits to only a handful of people who observed a different day of rest.

Admittedly, there are problems with the rule. It does not tell us what is compelling. We must still decide that. It does not give us a list of the really pertinent factors. We must still decide those. And as to its quantitative dimension, it produces a paradox. The state's compelling interest usually is lost when only a few "odd" people protest a law's operation. So said Sherbert. But if many protest, then the state has a greater interest in enforcing the law. For example: A few Sabbatarians in South Carolina would not hurt the state's unemployment insurance program. Therefore, the state had no compelling interest in its rule that discriminated against them. So, freedom of conscience could be allowed. But if there were many Sabbatarians, they might burden the state with claims like Sherbert's. That would automatically produce the compelling interest. Then freedom could be denied. This paradox makes it appear that the compelling interest rule in its quantitative dimension is useful for matters that concern only a handful. But should the law discriminate between "handfuls" and "crowds?"

The Prior Restraint Rule. In several religious freedom cases the Supreme Court used the phrase "prior restraint" in part of an opinion which held a state act unconstitutional. This is a rule of law borrowed from the language of free press cases. It faults the government for acting before an offense has been committed.

Remember *Cantwell* v. *Connecticut?* It concerned an ordinance which required that an official determine before issuing a permit whether a religious canvasser was involved in a bona fide religious cause. And *Kunz* v. *New York* concerned a police official who had power to deny a permit to those like Kunz who, during the ensuing year, planned to speak publicly on the sidewalks of New York.

To the Supreme Court these cases involved a muzzling of speakers prior to their speeches. Both possible fraud, raised in the Cantwell case, and possible breach of peace, raised in the Kunz case, could be handled later, the Court said, by criminal arrests under laws which did not stifle speech before the fact.

On this general rule of free religion most justices have

been agreed in principle if not on the facts of a certain case. It has been a rule which promoted liberty of expression.

The Balancing Approach. Perhaps it is fruitless to look for any single law of religious liberty. In these pages we have learned enough to know that judges have been unable to unite on one in spite of much sincere give-and-take in many cases spread over many years. What has happened in fact has been less the formulation of a rule than the development of an approach. The approach may be described as an effort to balance the several factors of a case. Both individually and collectively, justices seek to weigh all the factors. The factors are too numerous and too different in size or shape or density to be fit into a generally usable verbal formula.

A paragraph from a widely-used American government textbook may well sum up what we have sensed the Supreme Court does when it decides a religious liberty case.

Whatever the doctrines, doctrines do not decide cases—judges do. And judges are constantly searching and seeking and explaining; hence the Supreme Court may undergo doctrinal changes especially when it deals with issues that lack a national consensus. Doctrines are judges' starting points, not their conclusions; each case requires them to weigh a variety of factors. What was said? Where was it said? How was it said? What was the intent of the person who said it? What were the circumstances in which it was said? Which government is attempting to regulate the speech? The city council that speaks for a few people or the Congress that speaks for a wide variety of people? (Only a very few congressional enactments have ever been struck down because of conflict with the First Amendment.) How is the government attempting to regulate the speech? By prior censorship? By punishment after the speech? Why is the government attempting to regulate the speech? To protect the national security? to keep the streets clean? to protect the rights of unpopular religious minorities? to prevent criticism of those in power? These and scores of other considerations are involved. And there is the future question of how much deference judges should show to the legislature's attempt to adjust these conflicting claims. In short, no test has been devised that will automatically weigh all the factors.[8]

A Transitional Note

After reviewing the cases and after exploring the rules of law related to the free exercise clause, it might be assumed that some conclusion about religious liberty in American society might be in order. Not yet.

Standing before the free exercise clause in the First Amendment is the establishment clause. It is proper that these clauses stand side by side because historically and logically they are inextricably intertwined. Thus, we must examine the establishment cases before we arrive at any overall conclusions.

As we turn to these cases, however, we must always bear in mind that there is finally an overriding purpose for both clauses—the promotion of religious liberty under law.

Notes

[1] Philip B. Kurland, *Religion and the Law* (Chicago: Aldine Publishing Co., 1962).

[2] Paul G. Kauper, *Religion and the Constitution* (Baton Rouge: Louisiana State University Press, 1964), pp. 15–23.

[3] C. H. Pritchett, *The American Constitution* (New York: McGraw Hill, 1968), pp. 554–567.

[4] Leo Pfeffer, *God, Caesar and the Constitution* (Boston: Beacon Press, 1975); Richard E. Morgan, *The Supreme Court and Religion* (New York: The Free Press, 1972).

[5] Reynolds v. United States, 98 U.S. 164 (1878) (italics added).

[6] Martin v. City of Struthers, 319 U.S. 152 (1943).

[7] Jones v. City of Opelika, 316 U.S. 620, 621 (1942).

[8] James M. Burns, J. W. Peltason, and Thomas E. Cronin, *Government of the People, Basic Edition*, 9th ed. (New Jersey: Prentice Hall, 1975), pp. 140–141.

7

Drawing the Line
Between Church and State

Introduction

One of the United States' greatest contributions to the art of government was the idea and practice summed up by the phrase, "separation of church and state." That phrase, not found in the Constitution, is ambiguous. It or its equivalent has been used for centuries, describing arrangements that Americans denounce. And today that phrase is used in nation-states, like the USSR, to describe church-state relations that most Americans would say were the opposite of "true separation."

Perhaps we might do well to stop using the phrase entirely. After all, the Constitution does not use it. It only says that, "Congress shall make no law respecting an establishment of religion, or prohibiting the free exercise thereof." Notice, the words, "separation," "church," and "state" do not appear, let alone Thomas Jefferson's commonly used metaphor, "a wall of separation."

The problem of finding the correct term shows us that the American model of church-state relations did not spring fully grown from any legal phrase or metaphor. Rather, it slowly developed in the eighteenth and nineteenth centuries in the several states. Some states needed to disestablish their churches after the Revolution—a practice not completed until 1833 in Massachusetts. This disestablishment meant different things in different states, in part because Colonial establishments had differed.[1]

In a terribly oversimplified effort at summarization, the several state disestablishments made all churches into legally equal, private associations, lacking state legal aids, controls, and financial assistance. It removed from the established churches certain government functions like keeping birth and death statistics and ended their monopoly on performing marriages. And very slowly over the whole course of American history, the disestablishment of churches and religion came to mean less and less indirect government aids and supports for both churches and that general cultural religion that continues to have a very important place in American society long after all legal establishments have ended.

Until 1947, the federal government was far less concerned with conflicts over what the establishment of religion meant than were many states. True, it often did things that raised establishment questions, but these actions usually did not become hotly controversial. For example, it maintained the military chaplaincies and began each congressional day with prayers. Objectors to such practices were few and impotent. So federal officials rarely wrestled seriously with the niceties of church-state legal relations until this generation.

But beginning in the 1940s all three branches of the government in the nation's capital have been forced to consider and reconsider the meaning of the establishment clause. Congress, by passing several such measures as the Hill-Burton Act, which gave monetary aid to church-related hospitals and the Elementary and Secondary Education Act, which made available some indirect supports to parochial school students, was forced to debate that meaning. The administrators who developed the detailed regulations for such new laws did the same. And of primary concern here, the Supreme Court handled roughly a score of cases on establishment grounds. Most of these cases will be summarized or referred to in passing in this chapter. Together they will give us the best overview of what the prohibited "establishment of religion" means.

Government Can Benefit the Individual

The Supreme Court centered much effort on an establishment case in *Everson* v. *Board of Education* in 1947.[2] The effort produced less than final results, but it did give the nation a famous paragraph summarizing limits on the state, and it did develop a somewhat useful rule of law distinguishing between aid to religion and aid to persons.

Under a New Jersey law, a local school district provided that parents of all school children, including those enrolled in parochial schools, would be reimbursed for bus fares pupils spent on the way to and from school. Arch R. Everson regarded the payment to parents of parochial school students as an establishment of religion under the New Jersey and federal Constitutions. He went to court to stop the practice. He won in the trial court, but lost in the New Jersey Court of Errors—its highest tribunal. On to the federal Supreme Court he marched.

The Supreme Court took the occasion to say for the first time that the First Amendment's establishment clause was included in the sweeping words of the Fourteenth Amendment controlling the several states. This alone made the decision a landmark, for it gave a plaintiff a new and powerful federal lever against state actions that might be thought to establish religion.

On the establishment issue the vote was close—five to four. The majority opinion made the vote seem even closer. In it Justice Black set out the meaning of the words "no law respecting an establishment of religion." His tone was that of a strict separationist.

He concluded that the clause meant,

at least this; neither a state nor the federal government can set up a church. Neither can pass laws which aid one religion, aid all religions or prefer one religion over another . . . no tax in any amount, large or small, can be levied to support any religious activities or institutions whatever they may be called, or whatever form they may adopt to teach and practice religion . . . in the words of Jefferson, the clause against the establishment of religion by law was intended to erect "a wall of separation between church and state."

But then Justice Black changed his tone. In this case, he said, there was *no* unconstitutional state aid to religious institutions. The money spent was only an aid to the children—an individual benefit. Certainly, the state had power to provide for their safe transportation on dangerous streets. The fact that some were being transported to parochial schools made no difference whatsoever. Thus, while American law made for a wide separation of church and state, it did not and, indeed, could not prevent individuals from receiving equal treatment by the state. "We must be careful, in protecting . . . against state-established churches, to be sure that we do not inadvertently prohibit New Jersey from extending its general state law benefits to all its citizens without regard to their religious belief."

Justice Black, however, wanted to be sure that he was not misunderstood. This bus fare reimbursement program, he said, approached the "verge" of what was not permitted. Thus, he said yes to the program while seeming to mutter no.

In dissent Justice Jackson chided the majority for trying to face two ways at once. And he and the three other dissenters agreed that the majority had failed to understand American legal history respecting the separation of church and state. That history prohibited even this small, indirect aid.

Notice, one idea was accepted by majority and minority alike. A parochial school was regarded as a religious institution like a church. This was, of course, a very important assumption, and one that many people denounced. They had some reason. In 1899 the Supreme Court had decided that a hospital operated by a Catholic order was *not* a religious institution in the eyes of the law.[3] And, as we shall see in chapter 8, church-related colleges were later treated by the Court as if they were distinct from elementary and secondary parochial schools with respect to their religious qualities. Thus, there are two kinds of religious institutions when the meaning of the establishment clause is considered.

Justice Black lived to regret what others did with his Everson opinion in spite of his careful warnings about being on the "verge." In *Board of Education* v. *Allen*, 1968, a case arose over a New York state program which loaned textbooks on secular subjects to students in parochial and private schools.[4] Technically, the books were owned by the local school district, but in practice once they were delivered to the parochial school, they remained completely in its control. The case was followed with much interest by many groups because part of the groundbreaking federal Elementary and Secondary Education Act of 1965 provided funds for similar programs which made available learning materials to students in nonpublic schools. This federal program was yet to be tested in courts.

The initiation of the case involved a legal nicety. In New York, the ordinary person has a very hard time getting into court to challenge a regular state expenditure. The legal hurdle involved is called, "standing to sue," a matter that merits passing notice here as a warning to any who think that all one needs in order to challenge a government program is money to go to court. A local school board decided that since it probably had standing to sue, it would challenge the state law. Thus, a local New York Board of Education became the plaintiff alleging the New York law was unconstitutional

The trial court decided for the board on *both* the establishment and standing to sue grounds. The New York Appellate Division reversed on standing to sue alone. The highest New York court, the Court of Appeals, reversed the appellate division on standing to sue, allowing standing to the board, and then by four to three reversed the trial court on the First Amendment issues, saying the state program was constitutional. These flip-flops are also noted to give the reader a feeling for the closeness and complexities of many such cases.

Undaunted the local board of education went to the United States Supreme Court, perhaps hoping that Justice Black would write the majority opinion saying the schoolbook program for parochial students went beyond the "verge." But Justice White wrote instead, finding that schoolbooks were like buses—primarily of benefit to the student, not to the school. Thus, the

Everson decision became the rule of law that controlled in this case. New York had not established religion by the book loan program.

Justice White also found he could rely on other precedents. In the famous prayer cases, the majority had said that for a school program to pass the First Amendment's establishment test, it must have a "purpose and primary effect" that was secular. Since New York provided the students with none but state-approved secular books, this rule of law was also met. Indeed, the Everson "individual benefit theory" and the secular "purpose and effect rule" were found to mesh together and fit this case beautifully.

Justice Black and Justice Douglas dissented. The former thought he knew what Everson had meant, since he had written the opinion. Bus transportation was, to him, far different from loans of textbooks. Books were an integral part of the school's educational effort. That effort was aimed at religious ends. This program, then, unconstitutionally established religion. But Justice Black found that others had understood his 1947 words differently—not an unusual finding for judges who live a long time.

Government Can Benefit the Society

Just as a government program benefiting a person may incidentally benefit a religious agency, as in the Everson case, so a law benefiting the society at large may incidentally benefit some religious groups. Thus said the Supreme Court when it upheld the blue laws of three states against the claim that they improperly established the rest day of the "predominant Christian sects." [5] It also said, as described in chapter 5, that these laws did not infringe upon the religious liberty of Sabbatarians.

The opinion related to four separate appeals from three state courts. Though the state laws differed, all required the closing of businesses on Sunday. None allowed for the alternative offered by some states of closing on Saturday instead.

Those appealing the cases argued that, "Sunday is the Sabbath day of the predominant Christian sects" and that the "purpose" of making it a day of rest was, "to facilitate and encourage church attendance, . . . to induce people . . . to join . . . (these) sects, . . . (and) to aid the conduct of church services and religious observances."

In the two of the four cases that isolated the establishment issue from the kindred religious liberty issue, Chief Justice Warren disagreed with the appellants. He wrote for a majority of eight, receiving support from Justices Frankfurter and Harlan in a concurring opinion. Only Justice Douglas would have struck down the state laws.

The chief justice conceded that once Sunday closing laws were religious laws, designed to aid Christian churches. He explored Anglo-American history on this matter back to the year 1237. If aid to religion were still the purpose of these laws, then they would be unconstitutional.

But, he went on, the "purpose and effect" of such legislation today was secular.

In light of the evolution of our Sunday Closing Laws through the centuries, and of their more or less recent emphasis upon secular considerations, it is not difficult to discern that as presently written and administered, most of them, at least, are of a secular rather than of a religious character, and that presently they bear no relationship to establishment of religion as those words are used in the Constitution of the United States.

Throughout this century and longer, both the federal and state governments have oriented their activities very largely toward improvement of the health, safety, recreation and general well-being of our citizens. Numerous laws affecting public health, safety factors in industry, laws affecting hours and conditions of labor of women and children, week-end diversion at parks and beaches, and cultural activities of various kinds, now point the way toward the good life for all. Sunday Closing Laws, like those before us, have become part and parcel of this great governmental concern wholly apart from their original purposes or connotations. The present purpose and effect of most of them is to provide a uniform day of rest for all citizens;

the fact that this day is Sunday, a day of particular significance for the dominant Christian sects, does not bar the State from achieving its secular goals. To say that the States cannot prescribe Sunday as a day of rest for these purposes solely because centuries ago such laws had their genesis in religion would give a constitutional interpretation of hostility to the public welfare rather than one of mere separation of church and State.

The long concurring opinion of Justice Frankfurter also found that the state laws in question were secular. Even Justice Douglas' dissent conceded that more and more their secular quality replaced their religious quality. Yet, to him, the choice of Sunday played favorites, and favoritism the First Amendment's religion clauses forbade. Quoting a Washington, D.C., Protestant clergyman he asserted, "We do not have the right to force our practice on the minority."

In our nation the minority of sincere Sabbatarians, we may be sure, still is of that mind.

Government Cannot Promote Religious Education

In the nineteenth century many American public schools clearly had a Protestant bias. Many consciously supported, if they did not promote, certain religious beliefs by daily prayers, regular Bible readings from only the King James Version, and even by more or less regular appearances of local clergymen.

Slowly the public schools became more and more secularized. This movement was pushed in some places by Roman Catholics who disliked the Protestant overtones of public school religion, by Jewish groups, and by persons more or less offended by all religions.[6]

My own experience in the public schools of Moline, Illinois, in the 1930s and 1940s will show that this secularization of public education was very complete in some places well before the federal Supreme Court began acting on matters of religion in the classroom. In no grade was there prayer or Bible reading. Religious assemblies were never held. Nor were there religious education classes optionally available. History and literature classes never stressed religious topics. Even the grade school Christmas program was almost devoid of religious reference. Santa Claus, reindeer, and elves were its subject; "Twas the Night Before Christmas," its text. Perhaps, we closed with "Silent Night," but, if so, in fading memory it is drowned out by a more robust "Jingle Bells." Indeed, the single "religious" program I can recall was the graduation baccalaureate service held in the senior high school auditorium on a Sunday night. By the time I attended it, I knew enough to realize that the minister who gave the sermon was trying not to offend anyone on grounds of religious ideas. His text was: "Two prisoners behind prison bars. One looked at the sand; the other the stars." My Sunday School expertise told me that this was not even from the Apocrypha. And the substance of the sermon rested far more on Dale Carnegie than on Jewish prophets or Christian apostles.

Five years after that baccalaureate masterwork, the federal Supreme Court began making the education of all school children as secular as mine had been. The year was 1948. The case was *McCollum* v. *Board of Education.*[7]

The school board of Champaign, Illinois, at the urging of local clergymen set up an in-school religious education program. Students, with parental approval, could attend religious education classes once a week during regular school hours. Any religious group could offer classes. The teachers of these classes were chosen by religious groups and approved by school authorities. Pupils who did not want to attend stayed in school, engaging in other supervised activities. Vashti McCollum, mother of a school child, challenged the program on establishment of religion grounds. Losing in Illinois courts, she appealed to the Supreme Court. Interestingly, there she was supported by a joint Seventh-Day Adventist and Baptist Joint Committee on Public Affairs amicus curiae brief.

Justice Black, fresh from his labors on the Everson case, wrote the majority opinion which found that this program was an unconstitutional state support for religion. Perhaps, the most crucial sentences were these: "Pupils compelled by law to go to school for secular education are released in part from their legal duty upon the condition that they attend religious classes. This is beyond all question a utilization of the tax established . . . public school system to aid religious groups spread their faith."

Justice Frankfurter concurred, stressing the program's impact on children who belonged to the smaller sects which lacked resources to participate in a district-wide program. These children would be under "obvious pressure" to attend one of the religious classes and thereby be indoctrinated contrary to their beliefs. If they bravely opted out, they would experience a feeling of separation not desirable in the public schools. The justice's powerful paragraph on these effects of Champaign's "establishment" may show the utility of some religious balance on the Court. He was of Jewish background.

Justice Reed alone dissented, arguing that the long experience of American history more than the cold logic of constitutional phrases should be consulted on the meaning of the establishment clause. After all, such programs had been common in public education history for decades.

The decision brought a storm of angry protest. Inevitably, the Court would be forced to think the matter over again. "Again" came in 1952 in the New York City case of *Zorach* v. *Clauson*.[8]

New York's religious and school personnel had developed a religious education program that differed somewhat from the one just described. It released students from public schools for one hour a week if, with parental consent, they registered for privately conducted religious education courses held *off* school grounds. The sponsors of these courses kept attendance reports which they returned to school officials. Nonparticipating students had to remain in school. While there was a less direct relationship between the religious education program and the school officials here than in the McCollum case, the public school's authority was an ingredient in the program.

Many people found it hard to distinguish between the facts in the McCollum and Zorach cases. To them, the only real difference was whether the class was on or off campus. Yet, to the surprise of some, the Supreme Court upheld the New York plan. Justice Douglas wrote for a six to three majority.

The constitutional standard is the separation of Church and State. The problem, like many problems in constitutional law, is one of degree.

In the McCollum case the classrooms were used for religious instruction and the force of the public school was used to *promote* that instruction. Here, as we have said, the public schools do no more than *accommodate* their schedules to a program of outside religious instruction. We follow the McCollum case. But we cannot expand it to cover the present released time program unless separation of Church and State means that public institutions can make no adjustment of their schedules to *accommodate* the religious needs of the people. (italics added)

The words "accommodate" and "promote" set a tone different from the tone in the McCollum opinion. Further, Justice Douglas added,

The First Amendment . . . does not say that in every and all respects there shall be a separation of Church and State . . . Otherwise the state and religion would be aliens to each other—hostile, suspicious and even unfriendly.

We are a religious people whose institutions presuppose a Supreme Being. We guarantee the freedom to worship. We make room for . . . a variety of beliefs and creeds . . . We sponsor an attitude on the part of government that shows no partiality to any group and that lets each flourish . . . When the state encourages religious instruction or cooperates with religious authorities by adjusting the schedule of public events to sectarian needs, it follows the best of our traditions.

Dissents by Justice Black and another by Jackson, joined in by Frankfurter, were sharp. They argued that the New York program differed from the Champaign program in location only. This difference did not make enough of a distinction for the requirements of the establishment clause.

But that settled the matter for the Supreme Court. No other such case has been heard by it. Off campus, yes; on campus, no. That's the rule.

Government Cannot Conduct Devotional Exercises

The Supreme Court's prayer decisions in 1962 and 1963 caused much uproar in the land. So offended were so many people that proposed constitutional amendments intended to undo the decisions' effects occupied much time of the House and Senate before they were defeated in both. And each year such amendments get more or less serious treatment in congressional committees.[9]

The heated reaction is not so easily explained in light of American history. Some state courts had made similar decisions much earlier and no comparable reaction took place within those states. For example, in 1910 the Illinois Supreme Court declared that the voluntary reading of the King James Bible, the singing of hymns, and the recitation of the Lord's Prayer violated the Illinois Constitution.[10] That judgment did not remain an issue in Illinois politics, nor did it seemingly affect the quality of religious life in that state. Interestingly, in the 1960s Senator Everett Dirksen of Illinois led the attack on the Supreme Court decisions in the United States Senate. Had he succeeded in obtaining proposal and ratification of his federal prayer amendment, prayers in his own state's schools would still have been legally improper under his own state constitution!

The first of the prayer decisions came out of New York. There the New York Board of Regents had composed this prayer for the public schools. "Almighty God, we acknowledge our dependence upon Thee, and we beg Thy blessings upon us, our parents, our teachers and our country."

No New York school district had to use the prayer, but if a prayer were used in school exercises, this was the only option. Further, no student had to join the exercise. Participation was voluntary.

Some parents in a district using the prayer went into court for an order to end the practice. They claimed that the use of the prayer established religion and adversely affected religious freedom. While the New York courts had difficulty with, and were divided on, the case, they found the prayer constitutional. The parents appealed to the Supreme Court, and in 1962, *Engel* v. *Vitale* was the result.[11]

Justice Black wrote for the eight to one majority. Resting on the history of the establishment clause more than on a close reference to previous cases, he concluded that the First Amendment's establishment clause "must at least mean that . . . it is no part of the business of government to compose official prayers for . . . the American people to recite as a part of a religious program carried on by government."

The phrase "to compose official prayers" was unfortunate. It centered the attention of some on the fact that a state board had written and prescribed this prayer as the only prayer for New York schools. Therefore, people trying to find an escape from the decision concluded that the use of unofficial prayers might be acceptable.

The conclusion was obviously wrong, given the opinion as a whole. Justice Black had made it clear that; (1) such school prayers were religious activities, (2) government power could not be used for religious activities, and (3) even the voluntary aspect of the New York program did not redeem it. That is, his argument was aimed against *all* public school devotional exercises, even if his summarizing sentence seemed to tie it to the New York situation.

Justice Douglas concurred with an opinion that centered on the fact that the prayer improperly used state financial resources to aid religion. He was probably using the occasion to write about something not then before the court—financial aid to parochial schools. Excited judges occasionally commit this legal sin.

Justice Stewart dissented alone, stressing the long tradition of such prayers and the felt need of some people to join in public religious devotionals.

Before the Engel decision was handed down, the next two cases were well on their way to the same court. One, *Abington School District* v. *Schempp*, involved a Pennsylvania school district which had required Bible reading each day, followed by the Lord's Prayer. When that case started, participation by students was required. But before it reached the Supreme Court, the Pennsylvania legislature had made such devotionals voluntary. The other, *Murray* v. *Curlett*, came from Baltimore, Maryland, where a similar exercise was also shifted during the legal challenges from a compulsory to a voluntary requirement. The Maryland challenge was made by a publicity-wise atheist, Madalyn Murray O'Hare, who later organized the Society of Separationists to promote stricter church-state separation.

The two cases were joined by the Court. The 1963 result was the same as in the Engel verdict. It made no difference that the prayer was not written by a state board. The state could not engage in the practice of conducting religious devotionals.

Justice Clark wrote the majority statement for himself and seven others. He tried to clarify the meaning of the establishment clause with these words, which in less qualified form had first appeared in the Sunday law cases:

The test may be stated as follows: what are the purpose and the primary effect of the enactment? If either is the advancement or inhibition of religion then the enactment exceeds the scope of legislative power as circumscribed by the Constitution. That is to say that to withstand the strictures of the Establishment Clause there must be a secular legislative purpose and a primary effect that neither advances nor inhibits religion.[12]

The justice found it necessary to dispose of an argument that may seem curious to some. The two school districts had said that the Bible reading and prayer were not religious at all. They were only a secular program to teach morality. Clark viewed this as unrealistic, given the society's understanding of things. Such devotionals were obviously religious.

The conclusion of Justice Clark's opinion was aimed to

quiet fears. Religion, he said, held an exalted place in the nation. Schools may teach *about* religion, and they may not promote the religion of secularism.

Justices Brennan, Douglas, and Goldberg, while supporting Justice Clark's statement, wrote their own concurring opinions. Justice Brennan's alone ran for seventy-seven pages. Indeed, each of the three made different points and made them in ways which were distinct from Clark's effort—a fact which precludes summary here and which illustrates once more the ambiguity of the First Amendment.

Justice Stewart again continued his lonely dissent. One part of his opinion held that the issue of compulsory participation was central to the cases. Compulsion should be proved before the programs were struck down. No proof of compulsion affecting any child was shown in the record.

The debates over the 1962 and 1963 decisions still go on over a dozen years later. Otherwise law-abiding school officials in many school districts deliberately continue to violate the Supreme Court rulings. As noted, proposed constitutional amendments are offered each session of the Congress to move the prayer clock back to 1961.[13] Also, a bill was introduced into the Congress that would deny the Supreme Court the power to hear school prayer cases. Such a bill, of course, would require only a bare majority for passage, unlike a constitutional amendment.[14] State legislatures have passed measures providing for school prayer and meditation that seem to flatly contradict the Court's intent.[15]

One of the most interesting results of all is the growth of efforts to teach *about* religion in public schools. Justice Clark's opinion included this assertion:

It might well be said that one's education is not complete without a study of comparative religion or the history of religion and its relationship to the advancement of civilization. It certainly may be said that the Bible is worthy of study for its literary and historic qualities. Nothing we have said here indicates that such study of the Bible or of religion when presented objectively as part of a secular program of education may not be effected consistent with the First Amendment.

These words gave impetus to efforts to promote the objective teaching of religion in public schools within the already established curriculum or in newly established courses. The National Council on Religion and Public Education unites Catholic, Protestant, and Jewish groups in such an effort. Another organization, the Religious Instruction Association, has produced a "how-to" book for this purpose.[16] Thus, the prayer decisions are putting the fourth "R" into some classrooms.

This development has precedents at the college level of public education. There, many courses about religion are taught in literature, philosophy, sociology, and psychology departments. Indeed, a graduate degree in religion can be earned in some state universities.[17]

However, this movement may not be completely without legal challenges. Some groups fear that public educators cannot be objective about religion. Also, some people—religious and nonreligious—oppose even as objective a treatment of religion as any educator could develop. In 1967 the Washington State Supreme Court heard a case in which two churches asked that the University of Washington be required to stop teaching a course called, "English 390: The Bible as Literature."

The churches argued that the state was teaching the course in a manner "contrary to" their religious beliefs, and that the objective teaching of the Bible as literature was, "itself the presentation of a religious point of view." Therefore, the course violated the state constitution and both religion clauses of the First Amendment.

The trial court found the course to be objectively taught, saying, "There is no evidence that English 390 . . . is intended to affect the religious beliefs of students . . . or indoctrinate them in any particular religious belief or that it has had that effect."

The state supreme court accepted the trial court's finding on this point. It asked if the churches would have Milton, Dante, Handel, and other great works of literature and sacred music removed from the university curriculum? And it concluded in a brief opinion that these purely objective courses violated neither the state constitution nor the First Amendment.[18] But one justice dissented because he found such a course inevitably involved an attack on the ideas of many religious people.

The federal Supreme Court refused to accept an appeal from this decision.[19] But in a case that arose in Arkansas and reached the federal Court the same year, it had to face the issue of religious neutrality in public education from a different perspective. We now turn to that case.

Government Cannot Promote a Religious Doctrine

The establishment clause for all its ambiguity was meant to separate the federal government from the heated controversies of religious doctrine. From Roger Williams to James Madison, many early Americans argued that this new nation should use every effort to avoid becoming what many European states had become to their terrible hurt—the political defenders of a religious creed. In 1791 most who ratified the First Amendment thought that it would ensure against that prospect, at least for the national government. And so it did.

But as late as 1968 in *Epperson* v. *Arkansas,* the Supreme Court found it necessary to strike down a state law which proscribed the teaching of "the theory or doctrine that mankind ascended or descended from a lower order of animals." The justices did so because in their unanimous view, the Arkansas law rested squarely on a religious doctrine. "The overriding fact is that Arkansas' law selects from the body of knowledge a particular segment which it proscribes for the sole reason that it is deemed to conflict with a particular religious doctrine; that is, with a particular interpretation of the Book of Genesis by a particular religious group." [20]

After this assertion Justice Fortas buttressed the opinion with numerous quotations from several earlier cases all maintaining that federal and state governments must be neutral "between religion and religion and between religion and nonreligion." Further, governments had no power to protect "any and all religions from views distasteful to them." And then using a formula from a recent church-state decision, he found that the Arkansas law had a "purpose and primary effect" that was religious and therefore null and void under the Constitution. In short, the law was a religious law and the state was clearly forbidden to exercise religious powers.

While the decision was unanimous, there were three concurring opinions. Two by Justices Harlan and Stewart were very brief, adding little to what concerns us. But Justice Black wrote more. He found that the law had never been enforced in forty years and that Susan Epperson had launched the suit only from an abstract fear that it might be. This, he thought, might mean that there was no "justiciable controversy"—no true case. Further he suggested that the Arkansas Supreme Court in upholding the law had interpreted it so that evolutionary theory might be taught alongside of fundamentalist theory on creation. Finally he contended that the majority evaded a tough problem when it simply said the state must be neutral on religious matters. To many people the theory of evolution was believed to be flatly antireligious. How then could the society hope for neutrality in its schools?

Here Justice Black raised something of the same question just described in the University of Washington, "Bible as Literature Case." All education rests on fundamental assumptions—so fundamental that many of them are religious, even though their holders might not call them that. Can teachers from kindergarten to graduate school be expected to maintain a religious neutrality that other people of widely divergent beliefs agree is neurality? No. But can there be enough neutrality so that most religious people can accept the public schools? We are still finding out.

Government Aid to Parochial Schools

Since 1971 there have been ten Supreme Court decisions on government aid to parochial schools and/or their students that were decided squarely on the meaning of the establishment clause. Three other decisions have concerned aid to church-related colleges, and one other has interpreted how an education act of the Congress can be used to benefit parochial school students. Of the ten cases, two have the same title, *Lemon* v. *Kurtzman,* and the name "Lemon" appears in yet another. The name, "DiCenso," also appears in two as does "Committee for Public Education and Religious Liberty." To add to this confusing catalog, none of these opinions was unanimous, several having concurring opinions, and more than one dissenting opinion. Other related cases have been or soon will be appealed to the Court.

Obviously, with all this litigation, the nation is divided over the meaning of the establishment clause as it relates to parochial education. Obviously the Court is also divided on it. More important than either of those facts is this: The nation's divisions on the establishment clause are deeply felt. From East to West excited people and angry groups demand legislation that gives aid or denies aid to parochial schools and their students. Losing in the legislative halls, these people and groups have the money and inclination to go to court, hoping that the legislative loss is not final.

The issues in all this conflict cannot be summarized in any single case referred to above. But by using one of the cases, that has several dimensions, *Meek* v. *Pittenger,*[21] and adding brief comments on a few others, the outline of the conflict may be described.

Pennsylvania, having had two laws that aided parochial education struck down by the Supreme Court in 1971 and 1973, was reluctantly before the Court again in 1975. Its most recent effort at aid provided that textbooks on secular subjects could be lent to children attending elementary and secondary private and parochial schools. Also it authorized the loan of instructional materials and equipment directly to such schools. Further it provided that certain secular "auxiliary services," such as counseling, testing, speech and hearing therapy, and instruction for exceptional children, be provided by public school personnel in the nonpublic schools.

Sylvia Meek and others, supported by the American Civil Liberties Union, the National Association for the Advancement of Colored People, the Pennsylvania Jewish Community Relations Council, and Americans United for Separation of Church and State, went to court claiming that such benefits to non-public schools violated the establishment clause of the First Amendment.

At the special three-judge district court (such a court is organized to speed up appeals to the Supreme Court), Meek and her associates had both failure and success. The district court unanimously upheld the textbook loan program as constitutional. By two to one it also upheld the provision of the "auxiliary services" to nonpublic school children. It unanimously invalidated that part of the program which loaned instructional equipment to these schools if the equipment could be used for religious as well as secular education—for example, a motion picture projector.

Dissatisfied, Meek and her associates appealed to the United States Supreme Court. There they did a bit better from their perspective.

Justice Stewart wrote for a fluctuating majority. He began by stating the rule of law the Court felt bound to use for establishment questions. "First, the statute must have a secular legislative purpose . . . Second, it must have a 'primary effect' that neither advances nor inhibits religion . . . Third, the statute and its administration must avoid excessive government entanglement."

He added that these "tests" gave a "convenient, accurate distillation" of the Court's past work on the establishment clause. So they do, but, alas for simplicity and certainty, different judges interpret the words of the tests differently. Indeed, both majority and minority used these same words!

On the part of Pennsylvania law that related to the loan of textbooks, Stewart carried five judges with him. The loaned books were secular textbooks with a secular purpose and effect. The loan which was of primary benefit to students rather than to the nonpublic schools did not involve too much church-state entanglement. Here Stewart could point to solid precedent. As noted earlier, a similar New York book loan program had been upheld in *Board of Education* v. *Allen* in 1968.

But Justices Brennan, Douglas, and Marshall dissented on the loan program. For them Brennan said the entire program would create too much church-state entanglement. This was true, in part, because, "it is pure fantasy to treat the textbook program as a loan to students." The books, in fact, were ordered by the nonpublic school, stored on nonpublic premises when not needed, and handed out by the same school. Indeed, Brennan noted that the law at issue had titles such as, "Textbooks loaned to nonpublic schools."

For a different six-judge majority, Justice Stewart found that both the direct loan of instructional materials and equipment and the provision by public authority of personnel for the "auxiliary services" in nonpublic schools were unconstitutional. Why?

Stewart argued that the total aid involved in the materials and equipment loans was "massive" and that it benefited the nonpublic schools as institutions as well as the students. Most important, the materials and equipment could be put to religious uses. The "primary effect" might be religious. So, this part of the state law failed part two of the three tests described above.

As to the "auxiliary services"—the speech therapy, and so forth—Justice Stewart found that they failed the third test in two ways. First, the state's teachers who went into the nonpublic schools would have to be closely supervised to ensure that they did not foster religion. True, they would not be hired by the nonpublic schools, but in the religious atmosphere of the nonpublic schools some teachers might be tempted to support religious objectives. Thus, public supervision would be required. The supervision would become the forbidden church-state "entanglement."

Second, too much church-state "entanglement in the

broader sense" might result from the auxiliary services program. It could become a political football. At appropriation time, the state legislature would find itself involved in refereeing a contest between those from church-related schools pushing for more such services and those pushing for less. The establishment clause was devised to safeguard America from political fragmentation along religious lines. The Pennsylvania program might create such fragmentation.

As the reader could have guessed, here Justice Stewart picked up the support of Justices Brennan, Marshall, and Douglas who, as noted, had thought that even textbook loans were unconstitutional. But he lost the support of three others, Justices Burger, Rehnquist, and White.

Chief Justice Burger and Justices Rehnquist and White agreed with the majority where Brennan, Marshall, and Douglas disagreed. The former group found no problem with the Pennsylvania loan of textbooks to nonpublic school pupils. That was unquestionably constitutional. But they dissented with vigor from the majority respecting the state's loans of material and equipment and provision of auxiliary services. While the chief justice wrote one dissent and while White signed another written by Rehnquist, they were all agreed.

To them, all the Pennsylvania programs at issue had a secular purpose and primary effect and none involved too much church-state entanglement. The chief justice said that the majority opinion was a "denial of equal protection" rights of the Fourteenth Amendment. He also warned that the decision could only anger those whose consciences required a parochial education for their children. The poor among them were being forced against their conscience to send their youth to public schools because the costs of unaided private education were becoming prohibitive for many families. Would this mean less church-state tension in the society or more? Clearly, more!

Justices Rehnquist and White found the majority had created a trap for itself. In fearing that this or that state aid to nonpublic schools might possibly be used for religious purposes, the Court made excessive entanglement of state and church inevitable. The Court's ungrounded fear would force the state to supervise closely the programs it financed. Thus, there would be too much entanglement. To Rehnquist and White, fearful judges, not the state programs caused the problem.

The arguments of the justices are not all that merits study in this case. The tone of the opinions must be noted as well. Burger, Rehnquist, and White spoke heatedly for more accommodation of private education by the state. Brennan, Marshall, and Douglas spoke heatedly for more separation. Perhaps because of these clashing tones, Stewart, Powell, and Blackman spoke without a clear ring of conviction—at least, so it seems to me. Whether I am right with respect to tone, a three to three to three Court is not able to end the debate in the society on this matter. Such division lacks authority or finality.

In spite of this, a review of all ten Supreme Court decisions on state aid to parochial education decided on the establishment clause since 1971 shows a surprisingly clear result. The Supreme Court will accept only a very limited variety of parochial aids. These aids include: the loan of secular, state-approved textbooks,[22] the funding of standardized tests and test-scoring services, and the expenditure of funds for therapeutic guidance and remedial services performed by public employees for private school students with learning problems.[23]

But a majority cannot be mustered that will allow much more than this short list. Supplementary salary payments for teachers of secular subjects in such schools were forbidden.[24] So was the state purchase from private schools of specific educational services—for example, instruction in secular subjects for those schools' enrollees.[25] Neither could the state pay for the maintenance and repair of private school buildings and equipment.[26] Nor could it reimburse nonpublic schools for services that it required of them, like the keeping of health records and the giving of nonstandardized tests.[27] Clearly, direct payments to such schools are not acceptable to the Court.

What of indirect aids to the parents of children who attend

nonpublic schools? Again the high Court majority is separationist in outlook. It has struck down tuition grants and tax deductions for parents.[28] It did the same for a plan that paid a "Parent Assistance Authority" money that the authority then handed out to parents of children who attended nonpublic schools.[29]

Thus, in spite of the three-way split we noted in the 1975 Meek decision, the Court has a majority that demands a sharp separation of church and state respecting aid to private and parochial elementary and secondary schools. But consistency built on a house divided against itself three ways may not endure. Indeed, it would be a great surprise if it did.

Government Aid to Higher Education

Colleges are different from elementary and secondary schools. So says the Supreme Court when it applies the limits of the establishment clause to federal and state programs affecting higher education. The Court reached this position in 1971 in *Tilton* v. *Richardson*.[30]

Eleanor Tilton, a resident of Connecticut, went to federal district court challenging the operation of the 1963 Higher Education Facilities Act in her state. Under the act, state officials using federal money could give grants to colleges, including church-related colleges, for the construction of academic buildings. No building so financed could be used for sectarian religious instruction or worship. If it were, the school would have to repay the grant or a part of it that was proportional to a twenty-year period during which the government claimed an interest in the building. After the twenty years, the government disavowed any continuing interest, and the building could be put to whatever use the college alone saw fit.

Tilton's challenge was, of course, grounded in the establishment clause. To her this program was a direct financial aid to religious institutions—an establishment of religion—forbidden by the First Amendment.

Her argument sounded persuasive for two reasons. First, as we have just learned in cases decided that very same day, the Supreme Court knocked down state programs that aided elementary and secondary parochial schools in less direct ways. Second, in 1966 in *Horace Mann League* v. *Board of Public Works,* the high court of Maryland had declared a similar state program unconstitutional for three out of four colleges on the basis of federal Supreme Court decisions.[31] While the Supreme Court had not granted review in that case, many church-state experts thought it pointed the path for similar cases. It merits attention here.

The Maryland Court pioneered the path following a suggestion of Leo Pfeffer, attorney for the Horace Mann League. Some church-related colleges are really church-related. In every possible way they support their church and its religion. Other church-related colleges, to the contrary, pay little or no attention to either their church or its beliefs. When the state aids church-related colleges, it must distinguish between the former and the latter. No sectarian colleges can be granted aid, for that would be an unconstitutional subsidy of religion. The essentially secular, church-related colleges are really like public colleges. They can be given state aid.

The Maryland judges said that they had to look at several measures of the degree of church relatedness: What were the college's stated purposes? What was the religious composition of administration, faculty, and student body? How did the college interact with its founding church? What was the place of religious education in the curriculum? What were the *outcomes* of the college in terms of alumni careers? How did the local community view the college's religious commitment?

In *Tilton* v. *Richardson,* lawyers for the plaintiff, including Leo Pfeffer, approached the Connecticut case by asking these same questions. By the standards used in the Maryland decision all the Connecticut colleges were seemingly sectarian.[32] But the federal district court and the Supreme Court viewed the standards and the law differently—that is, five justices of the Supreme Court did. The four-judge minority disagreed in two separate opinions which stressed the sectarian quality of the colleges and the church-state entanglement caused by the grants. So, the case was a close one.

For the majority, Justice Burger wrote an opinion that, in part, stressed the differences between higher education and elementary and secondary education. Colleges were in their nature less religious in impact on students. Why? College students were less subject to indoctrination. College programs were usually less concerned with the promotion of the faith. And a sort of professionalism and academic freedom on college campuses worked against a simplistic religious indoctrination. Thus, aid to colleges could be treated differently from aid to lower level schools.

Did this mean that no college could ever have such a strong religious orientation that it would not be denied federal aid? Justice Burger, while discounting the "composite profile" the Maryland court had used, would not go that far. "Perhaps," he said, "some church-related . . . (colleges) fit the sectarian pattern the appellants describe." But not these Connecticut schools. They had a secular dimension adequate for government aid.

Because of these assumptions, Justice Burger could find no primary effects of the grants that were religious. He was sure the purpose of Congress in creating the grant program had been secular. Further, he did not think that government would be entangled with churches in an excessive manner as it supervised this simple once-and-for-all aid program.

However, the majority found one fly in the church-state ointment. It declared that part of the Higher Education Facilities Act unconstitutional which limited the government's interest in buildings financed by its grants to twenty years. The buildings would have worth beyond that time, and, thus, there could be no religious use of the buildings for a longer time than that. How long does the government interest continue? The Court did not give an answer.

The opinion and decision were much criticized. How could one justify direct aid to church colleges and no aid to church elementary and secondary schools? Are the levels of education all that different?

But aid to higher education was legally buttressed two years later in *Hunt* v. *McNair*,[33] which involved a South Carolina program of support for private college bonds. The state created an Educational Facilities Authority which, at the expense of participating private and church-related colleges, issued revenue bonds to help them finance construction of buildings used for secular purposes on their campuses. The state paid nothing for this program and it bought no bonds, but while the college made payment on the bonds, the state held title to the property.

Justice Powell found all this quite constitutional. The state's program was secular. The primary effect was secular, for the college, whose assistance was challenged, was not a sectarian school even though it was owned by the Baptist state convention. Nor did the program create an excessive church-state entanglement, though that possibility might exist if the college failed to pay off its debt. Such a hypothetical prospect was not before the Court, however. Powell's logic carried five other justices with him.

Justice Brennan wrote a dissent for himself, Marshall, and Douglas. To him the college was clearly sectarian. Also, he found too much church-state entanglement. Years of interaction were at issue while the bonds matured. This entanglement distinguished the case from Tilton. "The South Carolina . . . scheme as applied to this sectarian institution presents the very sort of 'intimate continuing relationship or dependency between government and religiously affiliated institutions' that . . . was lacking in Tilton."

But a minority is a minority, and since then other states have set up similar programs. In at least one, Minnesota, the state supreme court has found its program constitutional.[34]

The most recent college-aid case, *Roemer* v. *Board of Public Works*,[35] is noteworthy for two reasons: First, by a narrow five to four margin it upheld a Maryland program of annual

general grants to church-related colleges for use in secular programs—the most sweeping state-aid to church-related colleges
so far found to be constitutional. Second, the four-judge minority included Justice Stevens, who assumed the same strict separationist posture as Justice Douglas, whom he replaced. This
change of personnel, then, did not change the Court's factional-
ism on the meaning of the establishment clause.

Thus, the Court, while rather strictly separationist on the
issue of state aid to elementary and secondary parochial schools,
is by one or two votes accommodationist on the issue of such
aid to church-related colleges. Does such a dualism seem likely
to persist?

Other Establishment Cases

The catalog of establishment clause cases just presented
is very complete. Together with the Walz decision, discussed
in chapter 3, which upheld a state's property tax exemption
for churches, we have explored practically all full Supreme
Court opinions on the subject. One unanimous opinion was
bypassed because it seemed somehow archaic when settled
in 1961. It was *Torcasco* v. *Watkins* in which the Court struck
down that part of the Maryland constitution which demanded
that an oath stating belief in God be required of all public
office holders—even of a lowly notary public.[36]

Another case also bears mention here because it has been
said to show one means of getting around the Supreme Court's
decisions against aids to parochial schools. After Pennsylvania's
plan for the purchase of secular educational services from parochial schools was struck down in *Lemon* v. *Kurtzman*, 1971,
a second *Lemon* v. *Kurtzman* case had to be settled in 1973.
The state, of course, had contracts with parochial schools under
its purchase-of-services plan. Did the state owe the schools
money under those contracts up to the night before Lemon
(1971) was decided? Yes, said a divided Court in Lemon
(1973).[37] People must act as if a state law is valid until it is
declared otherwise. This reality must be recognized and pay-

ments promised before the program was ended by the Supreme Court were due.

Leo Pfeffer, a longtime and strong opponent of state assistance to parochial schools, argues that this case and related developments show that, "a game plan [has] emerged." The plan is this. State legislators will knowingly pass unconstitutional laws aiding these schools. Payments under the laws will be quickly made. Since the laws will be in litigation for some time—say two years—before being finally struck down, the payments will be the state's way of "illegally" assisting parochial schools. He sees the plan working in New York, Pennsylvania, Ohio, and Connecticut.[38]

Is Leo Pfeffer correct in this charge? Only a person who could read the minds of legislators and governors could really tell. Two months after the 1975 Meek decision struck down Pennsylvania's provision of "auxiliary services," such as remedial speech programs for pupils in nonpublic schools, the Pennsylvania legislature passed a similar bill. This may suggest that Pfeffer's assumption is right. However, the new bill differed from the old, unconstitutional measure in that it offered these services only off nonpublic school grounds.[39] Thus, another view of what is happening than Pfeffer's is reasonable.

Since we have learned that the difference between *on* school grounds and *off* school grounds can settle a case, this may well be the Pennsylvania government's sincere effort to locate that very fine line between proper and improper parochial aid. Because many legislators firmly believe the Court is too strictly separationist in outlook, we can expect them to keep pushing to find the maximum aid possible. Also, it might be supposed that different legislators have different motives on these matters. In any case, it seems unwarranted to say there is some master "game plan" unless other evidence is offered than Pfeffer's assertion. Certainly if a court sensed such a "game" were afoot, it could stop state payments under the new aid program until that program's constitutionality had been settled. Lawyer Pfeffer would be sure to urge exactly that, and he will be there to do it.

With all these cases now spread before us, it is time to ask if some general statement about the meaning of the establishment of religion clause is possible. Can we find a pattern hidden in the mosaic?

Notes

[1] A very complete history of this is found in Anson Phelps Stokes, *Church and State in the United States,* 3 vols. (New York: Harper and Brothers, 1950).

[2] Everson v. Board of Education, 330 U.S. 1 (1947).

[3] Bradfield v. Roberts, 175 U.S. 291 (1899).

[4] Board of Education v. Allen, 392 U.S. 236 (1968). The Supreme Court, when it struck down a state law aiding elementary and secondary church-related schools, has thought it necessary to invalidate the law completely. Thus the aids were also ended for private, nonreligious schools.

[5] The Sunday Closing Cases, 366 U.S. 420 (1961): McGowan v. Maryland; Two Guys from Harrison-Allentown v. McGinley; Gallegher v. Crown Kosher Super Market; and Braunfeld v. Brown. The establishment clause issue was raised most clearly in the first two cases.

[6] See Donald E. Boles, *The Bible, Religion and the Public Schools* (Ames Iowa; Iowa State University Press, 1961) and Richard B. Dierenfeld, Religion in American Public Schools (Washington: Public Affairs Press, 1962).

[7] McCollum v. Board of Education, 333 U.S. 203 (1948).

[8] Zorach v. Clauson, 343 U.S. 306 (1952).

[9] The bibliography on these matters is very extensive. All post-1964 books on the First Amendment's religion clauses are almost certain to spend much space on either or both the law and the politics of the issue. Besides the books already cited, one sharply critical of the Supreme Court's decisions may be added: Charles E. Rice, *The Supreme Court and Public Prayer* (New York: Fordham University Press, 1964).

[10] Ring v. Board of Education, 245 Ill. 334 (1910). This case is described briefly in Philip B. Kurland, "The Prayer Cases," Dallin H. Oakes, ed., *The Wall Between Church and State* (Chicago: Phoenix Books, 1963), pp. 173–174.

[11] Engel v. Vitale, 370 U.S. 421 (1962).

[12] Abington School District v. Schempp and Murray v. Curlett, 374 U.S. 203 (1963).

[13] For a summary of this, see Leo Pfeffer, *God, Caesar and the Constitution* (Boston: Beacon Press, 1975), pp. 202–227.

[14] Beth Hayworth, "Public School Prayer Issue Faces Congress," *Report from the Capital,* July–August, 1973, pp. 1,8.

[15] "School Prayer in Pennsylvania," *Report from the Capital,* February, 1973, p. 6.

[16] James V. Panock and Daniel Barr, *Religion Goes to School: A Handbook for Teachers* (New York: Harper & Row, 1968).

[17] See Anson Phelps Stokes and Leo Pfeffer, *Church and State in the United States*, rev. ed. (New York: Harper and Row, 1964), pp. 402–404.

[18] Calvary Bible Presbyterian Church of Seattle et al. v. Board of Regents, 72 Wash. 2d 912 (1967).

[19] Calvary Bible Presbyterian Church of Seattle et. al. v. Board of Regents, 393 U.S. 960 (1968), certiorari denied.

[20] Epperson v. Arkansas, 393 U.S. 97 (1968).

[21] Meek v. Pittenger, 421 U.S. 349 (1975).

[22] Board of Education v. Allen, 392 U.S. 236 (1968); Meek v. Pittenger, 421 U.S. 349 (1975); Wolman v. Walter 53 L. Ed. 2d 714 (1977).

[23] Wolman v. Walter, 53 L. Ed. 2d 714 (1977).

[24] Earley v. DiCenso and Robinson v. DiCenso, 403 U.S. 602 (1971).

[25] Lemon v. Kurtzman, 403 U.S. 602 (1971).

[26] Committee v. Nyquist, 413 U.S. 602 (1973).

[27] Levitt v. Committee, 413 U.S. 472 (1973).

[28] Committee v. Nyquist, 413 U.S. 472 (1973).

[29] Sloan v. Lemon, 413 U.S. 825 (1973).

[30] Tilton v. Richardson, 403 U.S. 672 (1971).

[31] Horace Mann League v. Board of Public Works, 242 Md. 645 (1966). C. Emanuel Carlson, "Court Decisions Rest on Nature and Function of College," *Report from the Capital*, June, 1966, pp. 6–7.

[32] See Pfeffer, *God, Caesar and the Constitution*, pp. 292–295.

[33] Hunt v. McNair, 413 U.S. 734 (1973).

[34] See Minnesota Higher Education Facilities Authority v. Hawk, No. 180½ (1975).

[35] Roemer v. Board of Public Works, 49 L. Ed. 2d 179 (1976).

[36] Torcasco v. Watkins, 367 U.S. 488 (1961).

[37] Lemon v. Kurtzman, 411 U.S. 192 (1973).

[38] Pfeffer, *God, Caesar and the Constitution*, p. 282.

[39] "Pennsylvania Again Provides Parochial School Aid," *Report from the Capital*, July–August, 1975, p. 7.

8
The Law of Church-State Relations: An Overview

Is There a *Law* of Church-State Relations?

Chapter 6 asked if there was a law of religious liberty—that is, was there a general principle or general rule the Supreme Court used in its disposition of religious liberty cases? Except for the most simple cases, we found no single principle. Rather, many were found that different judges used separately or in varied combinations as each thought proper for a given case.

Here we ask if there is a general legal principle or general rule for settling church-state controversies. The answer will be a bit different than before, for the Supreme Court has indeed fashioned two general principles, often stated as *tests*, which it currently uses, alone or together, to determine if the limits of the establishment clause have been overstepped by some government action affecting churches and/or religion. One of these principles is now so much used that it could be called dominant.

Yet the differences between our conclusions respecting the many-faceted law of religious liberty and the dominant law of church-state relations are not very important. While the Court can now point to one principle of church-state relations as determinative in *most* establishment clause cases, that principle is unclear. Different judges use it in different ways, disagreeing on its meaning. Therefore, we will conclude this chapter as we concluded chapter 6. The law is ambiguous.

The Law in Simple Cases

Again let us start with simple cases. For such, the establishment clause, while not self-defining, has clear legal meaning. Paraphrasing only some of Justice Black's words in the Everson case quoted earlier, the clause unquestionably forbids several things. These include any action by a state or the federal government that would: set up a church, aid one religion, prefer one religion over another, force anyone to attend or not attend a church, require the profession of some belief, involve open or secret participation in the affairs of any religious organization by government, and vice versa.

Hard as it is to believe, these simple limits are sometimes violated. Here are examples: local judges sometimes suspend a jail sentence if the criminal offender promises to attend church. In 1975, Jackson, Mississippi, donated one thousand dollars to help a Billy Graham evangelistic crusade in that city. Only after the American Civil Liberties Union threatened to sue did the crusade committee return the money. And for the same crusade, a National Guard general wrote a letter on official government stationery to all his troops inviting their attendance at the meetings.[1] Thus, even though the case is simple and the law is clear, some officials insist on using government in unconstitutional ways. As noted many times now, law and practice differ.

In paraphrasing Justice Black above, I deliberately left out two passages. The first of these said that under the establishment clause, government could not aid all religions equally. The justice is legally correct on this point. The Court has said so over and over again. However, this matter merits special comment, for it is still debated.

Some people read the words, "respecting an establishment of religion" as meaning only that no *single* religion and/or church can be given government aid or preference. They point out that after churches were disestablished in the new states, *all* were indirectly aided by tax exemption and almost all religions were aided by Sunday closing laws. Other examples can be cited. On the basis of these facts, some insist that a government's nonpreferential aid to *all* churches or to religion *in general* is proper under the First Amendment.[2]

But the Supreme Court has never given this view any support, except perhaps in a few incidental comments that can be mistaken to imply what was not intended by the whole opinion. Paradoxically, the most famous of these comments were the words of that strong champion of absolute church-state separation, Justice Douglas. In the *Zorach* case he wrote, "We are a religious people, whose institutions presuppose a Supreme Being" And, "When the state encourages religious instruction or cooperates with religious authorities by adjusting the schedule of public events to sectarian needs, it follows the best of our traditions."

But the whole of that opinion and case gives no support to the idea that government can directly assist *all* religions equally under the establishment clause. Justice Douglas was only trying to say that given one calendar in a society, time must be cooperatively shared between church and state. He commented that no government discrimination could be shown between "those who believe in no religion" and "those who believe." [3]

The nonpreferential aid position was decisively answered in the earlier McCollum decision. There the Court struck down a program which permitted churches to send teachers into the public schools for purely elective religious education classes. The program was designed to assist all religions which would and could cooperate. The lawyer for the school board argued that the establishment clause did not bar support for religious endeavors in general. Justice Black answered this position directly saying, "we are unable to accept" this contention.[4] And when Justice Douglas wrote the later Zorach opinion just referred to, he said he was following the precedent of the McCollum case.

Thus, the Court has always maintained that the establishment clause must be read as a prohibition of aid to *all* religions. But old legal heresies die slowly, and some who want government support for all religions still ignore a whole generation of contradictory law. So even some simple cases are not decided without heated argument.

The Law in Complex Cases

Another phrase from Justice Black's famous paragraph in the Everson decision was also omitted in my paraphrase above. The omission results from my feeling that by using the phrase the justice was trying to do the impossible. He tried to boil down the law of financial relationships between church and state into a single sentence. The sentence reads: "No tax in any amount, large or small, can be levied to support any religious acitivities or institutions, whatever they may be called, or whatever form they may adopt to teach or practice religion."

Here the discussion moves to more complex matters than something like a city giving a thousand dollars to an evangelistic crusade. Here we must begin to discuss those cases where several constitutional issues are simultaneously at stake, where the uncertain line between the sacred and the secular is drawn, and where the meaning of *church* and *religion* is obscure.

Justice Black's words concerning financial relationships are too brittle for these purposes. Read literally, they would put an end to the military and prison chaplaincies, and thereby put an end to freedom of religious exercise for some military personnel and prisoners. Read literally, they would treat a college which had only the barest historic connection with a religious group as if it were a church, and thereby violate our sense of reality. And the same would be said for a hospital that possessed some slight and noncontrolling tie with a denomination.

How could the justice write such words in the lead opinion in a crucial case? The answer brings us to the efforts of the Court at locating a general rule or principle by which to interpret the establishment clause in complex cases.

The Secular Benefit Rule. In the Everson opinion Justice Black announced a rule that still has validity and still may see some use. It is this: Where a government program is directed toward the secular benefit of individuals, there is no violation of the establishment clause if that program incidentally operates to give some benefit to religious agencies. Thus New Jersey could reimburse parents for the cost of bus rides their children took when going to parochial schools. This argument later justified the New York loan of secular textbooks to pupils of such schools.

Beyond bus rides and secular textbooks, the Court has refused to expand the "individual benefits" given to students, though efforts in that direction have been many. But the meaning of "individual benefit" is obviously loose enough so that this rule will still be used by those who seek government aid for some religiously sponsored enterprises.

Parallel to the individual benefit rule is the societal benefit rule found in the Sunday law cases. The state may give the whole society some secular advantage, like a uniform day of rest, even if many religious groups are thereby benefited in an incidental way.

Some judges while willing to use this rule for either the individual or the society will ask whether there is some alternative way of giving the desired secular benefit without aiding any or all religions. Thus the rule can be given a more separationist twist than first appears.

The Secular Purpose, Primary Effect, and Excessive Entanglement Rule. This rule evolved through three stages. It appeared in embryo in the Sunday law cases where Chief Justice Warren wrote only of a needed secular purpose and effect for the justification of any state program against the claim of an establishment of religion. Then in the prayer cases, Justice Clark gave it more detailed form as follows:

What are the purpose and primary effect of the enactment? If either is the advancement or the inhibition of religion then the enactment exceeds the scope of the legislative power as circumscribed by the Constitution. That is to say that to withstand the strictures of the Establishment Clause there must be a secular purpose and a primary effect that neither advances nor inhibits religion.[5]

Since Justice Clark found devotional Bible reading and prayer were religious, against two states' arguments that they were merely secular efforts at teaching morals, these exercises had both an unconstitutional purpose and primary effect. Out they went.

In cases since then, this rule has been used again and again, but, alas for simplicity, it has been expanded to improve its scope into its present and most authoritative statement.

Chief Justice Burger did not use the purpose and effect rule when he justified the grant of certain tax exemptions to churches in *Walz* v. *Tax Commissioners* in 1970. Rather, he pointed out that the establishment clause was intended to prohibit government sponsorship of religion. Tax exemption was not sponsorship, even if it gave some indirect assistance to churches. But he worried. What if a government program not involving sponsorship required a great deal of church-state entanglement respecting its administration? Then it could violate the establishment clause's limitations due to that "excessive entanglement" alone. So, as things developed in the 1970s, Justice Burger had tacked a third element on to the purpose and primary effect rule.

In its recent form, the rule reads, "First, the statute must have a secular legislative purpose . . . Second, it must have a 'primary effect' that neither advances nor inhibits religion . . . Third, the statute and its administration must avoid excessive government entanglement with religion." [6] Like so many sermons and chapter subheadings, three considerations must be weighed in the balances.

But we cannot rest with this statement of the meaning of the establishment clause, for, as noted earlier, while the justices all seem to like these words, they disagree on their meaning.

The Rule that Divides Rulers

Following Richard E. Morgan who wrote in 1974,[7] and confirming his ideas from the several opinions of the Meek case in 1975, it is necessary to divide the Supreme Court into three subgroups on recent establishment clause cases. Justice Douglas' retirement makes no difference to the division, for Justice Stevens, who replaced him, has also taken a strict separationist position. Each subgroup rested its opinions on the rule we have just described—that is, the secular purpose, primary effect, and excessive entanglement rule. The opinions all related to cases concerning state aids to church-related schools or their students. However, the judges' use of the rule may have wider application than this.

One group, the church-state "accommodationists," is composed of Justices Burger, White, and Rehnquist. They would use the rule in a way which would allow more aid to parochial schools than is permitted at present—potentially much more if the aid can be called indirect. For these three, aid to church-related colleges can be even more readily approved than aid for lower level schools.

Another group, the "superseparationists," is now composed of Justices Stevens, Brennan, and Marshall. They would use the same rule in a way which would give fewer aids than at present, throwing out the loan of secular textbooks to parochial students and some present programs that benefit church-related colleges.

The third group, the "moderate separationists," is made up of Justices Stewart, Blackman, and Powell. They have used the rule to find the status quo they helped create perfectly proper, accepting college aid programs and the loan of secular textbooks to parochial schools but rejecting other state benefits to such schools and their students.

For aid at the elementary and secondary level, both Justice Powell and Justice Stewart have written majority opinions.[8] It is hard to unite and summarize two opinions on two different cases without oversimplification, but let me try. Here is the synthesized joint position they hold.

The moderates apply the threefold establishment test quoted above to both *direct* and *indirect* aids to nonpublic

elementary and secondary schools. That is, they use the test
to strike down such *direct* assistance as loans of equipment
to these schools and supplements to teachers' salaries. To them
the primary effect of such aids must be regarded as aid to
religion. And if the state were to supervise the aid to ensure
that it had only a secular impact, too much church-state entanglement would result.

As to *indirect* aids, such as tax credits or tuition grants,
the moderates treat these as a sort of subterfuge. Do not these
benefits really run from the state straight through the parents
to the parochial school? Since that is actually what happens
according to the moderates, such *indirect* aids have a primary
religious effect. These indirect aids support the school with
its religious reason for being. One commentator has called this
the "conduit theory." [9]

Further, the moderates fear two levels of entanglement.
One is at the school administrative level. The other is at the
level of state politics. Both direct and indirect benefits to religious elementary and secondary schools must be denied if they
might create religious politics within the state, with a "more-
aid party" opposing a "less-aid party" in elections, the legislature, and in the administrative branch.

Since 1973 it has been clear that the accommodationists
use the threefold test more narrowly. Chief Justice Burger
would apply it only to *direct* aids such as supplements to teachers' salaries. It need not be applied to tax credits to parents
of parochial school students or to tuition grants to them. Such
indirect aids are clearly constitutional. The accommodationists
remember how the GI Bill worked to pour students with their
tuitions into any college or seminary. They might well accept
a similar state plan for parochial schools. Thus they might support very substantial state assistance if it were indirect.

The accommodationists fear church-state entanglement
only at the administrative level of education. Unlike the rest
of the Court, they do not see reason to fear church-state entanglement in the political sense—that is, a "more-aid party" fighting a "less-aid party" in the legislature. Indeed, they argue

that by not giving enough aid, the majority of the Court is causing the present parochial aid politics we now have in some states.

The superseparationists find that the primary effect of almost all indirect aid is religious and that excessive entanglement abounds when the state assists private elementary and secondary students. They can most properly use Jefferson's metaphor of a "wall of separation" to describe the establishment clause. Interestingly, they now are led by Justice Brennan, the Court's only Catholic.

Thus, the threefold test has three distinct meanings for the lower levels of education and more meanings for higher education. Need it be said that in the interpretation of the establishment clause the *who* of the judicial formula is far more important than the *what* of the judicial formula?

We can again note that our slogans which say we are governed by law rather than by men are wrong in important measure.

Notes

[1] "Billy Graham Crusade," *Report from the Capital,* September, 1975, p. 8.

[2] See for example, Charles E. Rice, *The Supreme Court and Public Prayer* (New York: Fordham University Press, 1964) and James O'Neill, *Religion and Education Under the Constitution* (New York: Harper and Brothers, 1949).

[3] Zorach v. Clauson, 343 U.S. 360 (1952).

[4] McCollum v. Board of Education, 333 U.S. 203 (1948).

[5] Abington School District v. Schempp and Murray v. Curlett, 374 U.S. 203 (1963).

[6] Meek v. Pittenger, 421 U.S. 349 (1975).

[7] Richard E. Morgan, "The establishment Clause and Sectarian Schools," Philip B. Kurland, ed., *The Supreme Court Review, 1973* (Chicago: Chicago University Press, 1974), pp. 57–97.

[8] Justice Powell wrote the opinion in Committee v. Nyquist and Sloan v. Lemon, 413 U.S. 756,825 (1973); Justice Stewart wrote the opinion in Meek v. Pittenger, 421 U.S. 349 (1975).

[9] Virgil C. Blum, "The Supreme Court and Religion," *Vital Speeches* 40:11 March 15, 1974, p. 339.

9
Religious Liberty Today

The Realm of Freedom

Our study of the many Supreme Court cases on religious liberty does not give an overview. In those cases, the Court drew a line between the permitted and prohibited. The line-drawing was difficult because for the most part only difficult cases reach our highest court. Focusing attention on the line leaves us with only a knowledge of, as it were, the twists and turns of a rocky continental divide. We might spend much time looking at this or that ridge of the divide, puzzling why it is here, while a short way off another ridge of only slightly different composition faces another way at right angles. But the composition of the ridge and its compass reading cannot tell us about all that spreads downhill to the right and to the left of the divide. We must look up and out for that.

Taking a practical, as well as a legal, view of religious life in this land, it is obvious that the realm of freedom is vast. Daily observation shows that American religion in many shapes, substances, and qualities—from high church worship to store-front gatherings, from prophetic reformism to pietistic with-drawal, from scholarly reflection to evangelistic fervor, from tightly knit denominationalism to complete localism—is active in a myriad of groups and programs. It speaks its many minds, sings its many songs, does its many good works, builds its many agencies, and fills its many treasuries with little government hindrance.

Regretfully, some of the American public aided by local

officials have not always supported this wide a realm for freedom. Chapter 4 told how Jehovah's Witnesses were persecuted in the late 1930s and early 1940s. Clearly, the realm of freedom is as large as it is because the law proved effective against those persecutions. The Supreme Court used the First Amendment to protect and enlarge the realm against ugly forces that would have made freedom's domain much smaller. Perhaps, the persecution of the Witnesses was a turning point in our history.

Since that sad time, whenever some government unit has set limits on religious expression, the Supreme Court has been willing, almost eager, to scrutinize those limits to see if they unnecessarily restrict the liberty the First Amendment promises. The Court has been libertarian in most matters, striking down what it thought were improper restrictions on freedom and thereby warning other government agencies, federal and state, not to attempt similar limitations.

Readers must judge for themselves the quality of the Supreme Court's work. But in my view, the cases found in chapter 4 show that the Court usually was willing, if anything, to err on the side of freedom—the only proper side on which to err in a free land.

Recall, for example, that it forbade what four judges argued was a most reasonable, secular peddler's tax, when that tax was applied to sellers of religious literature. Remember that it overturned an ordinance forbidding door-to-door canvassing, though the city said it was trying to protect the sleep of wartime night workers. Minority justices, in both cases, could assert that these were trivial and completely secular regulations, that they were clearly within state power, that they limited only slightly one of many means of expressing religion, and that the governments involved had several good reasons for adopting the limits. Nonetheless, the majority declared these trivial restrictions unconstitutional. And think again how the Supreme Court stretched the meaning of "conscientious objector" so far as to include an atheist under words that originally were carefully chosen to exclude such a person.

Further, when the Supreme Court set limits on the liberty to express and practice religious ideas, it did so only where governments had an undoubted power to act and where consensus in the society was overwhelming. A required smallpox vaccination in a day when that disease was a scourge, a mandatory parade permit for a crowded business district, an enforced child welfare law designed to protect against exploitation, and an altered income tax classification for a group that advertised candidates for public office—such examples of government powers exercised in spite of the claims of conscience seem understandable to most people and all but inevitable in modern society. Granted these are limits on freedom and granted such government actions will be thought of as unjust and unneeded by some. But government is designed to achieve some common good, some general welfare. In a nation where "freedom's ferment" has both produced and received from abroad a wonderful variety of religious groups, many government programs will be regarded as religiously unacceptable to some people and associations. On balance, freedom of religion has been given a sweeping range. The First Amendment has fulfilled its promise for the most part.

The Realm of Unfreedom

But let us not be too satisfied as we survey the large realm of freedom won and held. We must remember the losers just mentioned—those whose claims we reviewed in chapter 5. Even if to most people their causes seem wrong or, perhaps, silly, the very fact that they pressed them to our highest court shows that they cared deeply about what they thought were deprivations. It is sobering to think of the religious freedom claims lost in county and federal district courts and administrative agencies each year. A list of these would include disputes concerning state and local health measures that someone finds an offense to conscience; fire and zoning regulations that control the building of churches, schools, and hospitals; slum clearance project rules which are designed to control land use in a rigid way; child custody laws which may or may not consider the religious preference of parent or child; state university directives concerning the use of space for the convenience of campus religious groups; Federal Communications Commission regulations for radio and TV broadcasting.

Since governments are still expanding their functions, this list may very well grow. And if the recent, more radical lifestyles of some religious people, communes, and groups take permanent hold in the land, the list will certainly grow.

Yet it should be clear that a long list of grievances does not necessarily mean that religious freedom here is not broad. The long list can very well be a product of the broad freedom we enjoy. It is *because* we have much religious freedom that the Native American Church in the Southwest demands that it can use peyote as a sacrament. It is *because* we have much religious freedom that a few Jehovah's Witnesses demand exemption from jury service on religious grounds. It is *because* we have much religious freedom that Appalachian cults can demand the right to pass rattlesnakes around meeting halls as tests of faith.

The borders of freedom's realm are like the circumference of a circle. As the diameter grows, the circumference grows at a multiplied rate. I have heard a Native American argue that he could catch salmon in the Columbia River watershed as he saw fit, regardless of any limiting game laws, because the taking of salmon was an integral part of his religion. No one would make such a claim in a land where freedom of religion was sharply limited. The very claim shows the breadth of that freedom.

Contested Territory

Yet in spite of what has just been said, anyone who claims to love liberty cannot be passively content with a great realm of freedom spread out in one direction if some people argue that an area of unfreedom, completely unnecessary, is found in another direction. A free person and society will always attend to the task of increasing liberty's range, if possible, for two reasons: first, because of their commitment to freedom; second, because broadening liberty may reduce some of that society's frictions and angers. The question should always be this: Can we find some way of accommodating the demand for this or that freedom that will not harm people and the social order? For example: Granting that passing rattlesnakes around a meeting is dangerous, should it not be allowed if the meeting is composed only of adults who know the nature of the meeting and its danger? [1]

Let us look at three demands for religious liberty that produce much tension in America today and ask if there are ways in which this tension might be reduced.

The Military Draft. One realm of unfreedom that still exists in our society is created by the military draft law. Its population varies with the situation the nation faces. In World War II its numbers were relatively low, though by the end of that war one of every six federal prisoners was held for violation of the draft act. By 1974 its numbers were relatively much higher, scattered into foreign lands. [2] The end of the Vietnam War and the draft, the grant of a limited amnesty by President Ford, and of a pardon by President Carter have made the tensions related to this matter less noticed. But the nation has faced these tensions since the pre-Independence days of the Indian wars, and in a world of severe international rivalries their presence will not be forgotten.

One reason we will not forget is that there is in Washington, D.C., a lobby of the "peace churches." The Quakers have pushed politically to protect people from compulsory military service for over two hundred years. Presently, they are represented in Washington by the Friends Committee on National Legislation and the American Friend's Service Committee. Other "peace churches" are also present there or send representatives to the capital at crucial times. In recent years these have enjoyed support from other groups including the ACLU and the National Council of Churches.[3]

The argument of those pushing for more freedom for the conscientious objector commonly has two dimensions. First, it is argued that a broadened definition of CO status is required. Second, it is asserted that the status ought to be made a First Amendment right rather than, as at present, only a legal privilege.[4] In thumbnail form the logic goes something like this: The First Amendment protects freedom of religion and conscience.[5] Many people sincerely believe on grounds of religion and/or conscience that it is morally wrong to participate in military activity in some forms. Since freedom of religion insulates other people from the impact of other laws, conscientious objectors should have exemption from those forms of military training and service which offend them. As exemption has long been recognized in statutory law in inadequate ways and as the nation has not suffered from its past grants of CO status, it is time that Congress and the courts treat conscientious objection as a broad, fundamental, First Amendment right. Two distinguished judges have already led the way. Charles Wyznaski, Chief Judge of the Federal District Court in Boston, raised CO status to the constitutional level in 1969.[6] And Justice Douglas did the same thing in his dissent in *Gillette* v. *U.S.* 1971.

Whatever the adequacy of this argument, it is not likely to be adopted as American policy by the Congress or the Court in the near future. Congress has always acted with great caution when pressed to liberalize the law. Indeed, congressional adjustment of the draft law is viewed with foreboding by many in the "peace churches" for fear that new legislation will be less generous than the old. Further, the Supreme Court stopped marching in the liberal direction it had been headed toward in interpreting the law when it refused to allow exemption for "just war" objectors in the Gillette case.

These observations would seem to imply that this realm of unfreedom is likely to remain in our society unless a very unpopular war reinstituted the draft and changed thinking drastically. What then can a person do who wants to reduce the size of this realm? Do the long, quiet work of education in the society and its many subgroups that is still needed on this subject. People need to be told of the moral seriousness of many of the objectors, of the fact that many accept noncombatant service, of the assignment to "alternative service" that others are required to accept at no gain to themselves, and of the harsh experiences of the thousands in jail and exile who object in ways not covered by present law. Further, they need be reminded that the CO is a different person than the criminal deserter or the casual AWOL draftee. And, surprisingly, congressmen, who should already know all this, must be told the same things.

But make no mistake about optimism. This realm of unfreedom is likely to lurk in the background of the national mind into the unforeseeable future. It will emerge in our consciousness to plague us again if ever the draft is revived. Would it not be better to settle this issue in the quiet of peace than in the turmoil of war? The CO would be more apt to receive more generous treatment when others were not angered by the passions of military conflict.

Aid to Church Schools. Without question the most hotly divisive issue related to religious liberty in the United States today is the matter of government aid to church-related education, especially elementary and secondary education. Many people, including some who do not send their children to non-public schools, argue that there is a crucial limitation on *religious* freedom in this nation. Parents who want their children educated in schools which are organized around religious ideas find that they must pay heavily for this right. To them, the victory that private schools won in *Pierce* v. *Society of Sisters* was hollow. True, it protected the right of private schools to educate to meet state education requirements, but in practice this protection did not give meaningful educational freedom. Why not?

In compact form the legal argument runs as follows.[7] All

taxpayers bear the cost of public education. This is proper in modern society that requires much education for its well-being. Public education for legal and practical reasons must be secular. The Supreme Court has said so in several cases, and the society is so divided in religious outlooks that it cannot be otherwise. But for many people secular education is inappropriate to their deepest religious instincts. They require a religiously oriented—often called "God-centered"—schooling for their children. This means that public education, which they help pay for, cannot serve their needs.

When they send their children to church-related schools, they find they must pay the costs of those schools or their church must do so by raising funds for them. Very little government aid goes to such schools, even indirectly. For many of the poor, this puts church-related education out of reach. True, they have a legal right to it. Yet a right that costs so much cannot be exercised. Since by law they must send their children to school, they are forced to educate them in public schools whose approach to education violates their religious insights. For those not so poor or for those who are well-off, this means a special financial sacrifice because they pay twice for the society's education: once through taxes and once through tuition. This is unjust—a denial of equal protection of the law.

This disregard for the educational freedom for the poor and for equal protection for those able to pay private school tuitions is all unnecessary under the First Amendment. That amendment only says there shall be no "establishment of religion." It does not call for an absolute separation of church and state. The Supreme Court majority has been wrong in destroying many state programs of aid to nonpublic education. It could have found them perfectly constitutional as its minority has done repeatedly.

At least the Supreme Court could have accepted those state programs, like that of New York, which gave a tax deduction to parents of children who attended nonpublic schools. Such a deduction or, better, a tax credit—say $150 for each child—would not be a state payment to the school. Primarily, it would be a benefit to the parents, only secondarily affecting the school. The Supreme Court upheld individual benefits in the Everson case. It could do so for some form of tax credit just as logically.

Also, while church-related schools have a religious orientation, much of the education they give is identical to the secular education of the public schools. Church-related schools, after all, must meet state educational standards, educating in fundamental skills and for good citizenship. Ought not at least indirect aid be given to private schools on the strength of this nonreligious component of their total activity? This could be justified under the Supreme Court's doctrine that the state can support programs that have a secular purpose and primary effect.

Indeed, the Supreme Court's secular purpose and primary effect rule *requires* that parochial schools be aided. In its most authoritative statement it reads, "If either (the purpose or primary effect) is the advancement or the inhibition of religion then the enactment exceeds . . . legislative powers." [8] Present restrictions on state aid to parochial schools inhibit the religious inclinations of those who prefer such schools on grounds of religious belief. The state, therefore, must end this inhibition by assisting parochial education.

Another legal argument for such aid rests on the Walz opinion. In it eight justices upheld the constitutionality of property tax exemption for churches, certainly an indirect benefit for religion. That indirect benefit was said to be unlike a forbidden subsidy of religion. Why does the Court not treat indirect aids to parochial schools in the same way?

Beyond these arguments based on the definition of religious liberty and church-state relations, there is the argument which stems from the equal protection clause of the Fourteenth Amendment. That amendment forbids that states treat individuals differently when they are in identical situations. The parent and child of the nonpublic school are meeting state education requirements just like their counterparts of the public school. This requires that the state give them the same financial support. Pushed harder all the time, this argument could require dollar-for-dollar equality in all but the purely religious aspects of church-related education.

Surprisingly, given Supreme Court opinions, other branches of the federal government have shown the way on private school aid. They appropriated and spent multiple millions on education after World War II by giving each veteran money for tuition to any accredited college and seminary. This was done to benefit the veteran. The fact that it decisively increased enrollments in church institutions was not regarded as an establishment of religion. And in the Elementary and Secondary Education Act of 1965, Congress adopted the individual-benefit doctrine of Everson as it provided federal aids for students in both public and private schools. Other illustrations of federal programs benefiting private schools and colleges abound—for example; school lunch payments, college housing loans, and scholarship and research grants.

When made by some people, Catholics and non-Catholics alike, the argument can take a bitter turn at this point. Since by far most nonpublic elementary and secondary education is Catholic, and since Protestants have chosen to invest their educational dollars in higher education, it is asserted that the wide church-state separation demanded by the Supreme Court and many people for only the lower levels of education is in part a product of anti-Catholic bigotry. How else can one explain why colleges which may be clearly religious can get federal and state financing for whole buildings while parochial schools cannot get a motion picture projector from state government funds?

Feelings on this contrast of treatment are very deep, and given American religious history, including the history of Protestant domination of the public schools in the nineteenth century, they are understandable.

The point is mentioned not to scratch one of our nation's

wounds. Rather, it is mentioned to help show that this charge of unfreedom is one that is felt very keenly. Rightly or wrongly, many people argue vehemently that the First Amendment as interpreted by the Supreme Court discriminates against Catholics. One nationally-known Catholic writer, Virgil Blum, calls the Supreme Court's position "a degrading insult" to Catholics. He says some justices are "deeply passionate and hostile" to Catholics when they take up school aid issues. And he applauds a state judge who decided for tax credit aid to parents of parochial pupils for distinguishing between "freedom and tyranny." [9]

Were he alone or only the spokesman of one offended group, such feelings might be shrugged-off as inevitable in our pluralistic society. He is not alone. Other writers of national reputation, while using less strong terms, explain the lack of aid to parochial schools and the posture of the Supreme Court and society on this matter in large part in terms of the legacy of American anti-Catholicism. These include non-Catholics: for example, Wilbur G. Katz, a prominent Protestant and professor of law at the University of Chicago, writing in the *Atlantic Monthly;* [10] Will Herberg and Milton Himmelfarb, Jewish scholars and authors, writing in *Commentary.* [11] Indeed, they supply some useful ammunition for Professor Blum.

Whatever the validity of this charge, there are active pressure groups pushing for reinterpretation of the establishment clause so that more parochial aid might flow. Perhaps most visible of these is Citizens for Educational Freedom which publishes a monthly, *Freedom in Education,* and lobbies at state and federal capitols. A layperson's organization of well over 100,000 members who are about 90 percent Catholic, its considerable, if short-lived, successes have been scored in a few Eastern and Midwestern states in both legislatures and state courts. Also, the United States Catholic Conference which represents Catholic bishops, the Knights of Columbus, and the National Catholic Educational Association supports this general cause in less conspicuous ways. Some spokesmen for Orthodox

Judaism have also called for nonpublic school assistance as has a small but prominent Protestant magazine, *Christianity and Crises*.[12] Thus, this movement is not narrowly based.

But what of the other side of this legal argument? It too finds a broad base of diverse supporters, and its adherents are also moved by deep feelings and by a demand for religious freedom.[13]

Those opposed to aids for church-related schools at the elementary and secondary level usually begin their argument by pointing to state constitutions and to the accumulated federal and state case law on the matter. Many state constitutions are quite clear. State funds cannot be given to religious institutions. And scores of state court opinions interpreting state constitutions have been restrictive of even indirect aids to such schools if they allowed it at all. Further, from Everson in 1947 to Wolman in 1977, the federal Supreme Court has permitted only the indirect aid of bus rides, secular textbooks, provision of some therapeutic services, and payment for standardized testing at the lower levels of education.

Therefore, the argument goes, the law is settled and well-known on the matter. Granted this or that small point may be in dispute and granted here or there some justice wrote some fuzzy words, but the American people and their legal system have decreed that "no establishment" means no direct aid and little indirect aid to elementary and secondary church-related schools. Freedom of religion does *not* mean the right to government support for these schools. True, some people have theories to the contrary, but theories are not the law of the land.

When the antiaid argument is moved beyond this foundation, its supporters often center attention upon religious liberty. They say that there is religious freedom *not* to be taxed to support religious agencies and religion. Certainly, one of the major thrusts of both the antiestablishment and religious freedom clauses is that no one can be taxed to support any religion—his own or someone elses. Justice Black's Everson statement is recited, "No tax in any amount, large or small, can be levied to support any religious activities or institutions, whatever they might be called, or whatever form they might adopt to teach or practice religion." [14] While these words were from an establishment case, they have relevance for freedom of religion. Americans want to be free from any tax that aids religious endeavors.

And, it is argued, parochial schools are religious institutions. They are set up precisely for the promotion of religion and the churches that sponsor them. They advertise their programs as "permeated" with religion. It is "God-centered" education, as its supporters say. Even in its more secular dimensions, that education aims to tie all learning to a theistic world view, to divine revelation.

Since parochial education is religious in content and since its purposes are religious, what matter that it provides the same secular subjects required in public schools? Those secular courses are set in a religious context in the classroom and in the school as a whole. Taxpayers ought not and cannot be required by law to support this under either or both First Amendment clauses.

Importantly, government is not obligated to support people so they can better exercise their rights. The right of property does not require that a person must be given some. The right of a free press does not mean that governments must finance the writing and mailing of anyone's editorials. Further, in this connection, it is idle to say that these illustrations are inappropriate because state law requires that a child go to school, while it does not require that someone own property or write editorials. School attendance laws have long been obsolete for all but a very few people. Parents, not the state, require that children go to school.

Admittedly, the general ideas of the society about what rights mean have been changing. More and more Americans accept the idea that some rights need government support. For example, there is for all practical and legal purposes a "right" to social security of some sort. But a demand that freedom of education means state support of religious schools is not to be treated like some other demands for state aid. Why not? Because the antiestablishment clause was put in the Bill of Rights to end all state support of religious agencies.

This point, it is urged, must be stressed. True, freedom of religion is constitutionally required. True, freedom of religious education is constitutionally protected. The second clause of the First Amendment demands this. But the first clause, just as important, says that the state must not aid religion. Clause two does not override clause one. Thus, "educational freedom" does not require that the nation abandon its commitment to antiestablishment or antisupport of religion.

Further, it is a fiction that state tuition grants and tax credits are merely aid to parents, not aid to church-related schools. The state legislatures that set up such grants are consciously trying to aid these schools. Everyone knows it. By such programs the state singles out a class of people—parents of children in private schools, over 90 percent of which are parochial schools—for special economic benefits. They are singled out so that the schools they use can be benefited. The parents are mere conduits.

But what of the many exceptions to the strict separation of church and state in American history? Those who make antiaid arguments differ in their responses to this point. Some say all exceptions were errors, why make more? Others say that many or most recent or continuing exceptions can be explained. Payment of chaplains in the military or in prisons is the only way to ensure that people in unique places—military bases and prisons—can have any group religious expression at all. And the G.I. Bill that gave veterans money for tuition in colleges and seminaries originally met the special requirements of a nation that had dislocated millions of young people for several years. The nation had to use all its educational resources to return these people and itself to normal as quickly as possible. Such unique programs are not good precedents for permanent government aid to church schools.

What of the argument that the denial of aid to parochial school students is a denial of equal protection of the laws as required by the Fourteenth Amendment?

First, the antiaid debaters say the state provides equally for all in its public schools. Second, if anyone by choice places themselves in a burdensome situation, it is not the state's duty to remove that burden. The Supreme Court has said that freedom of religion may cause burdens for some people. Sabbatarians are hurt by Sunday closing laws, but that does not make those laws unconstitutional if the state's secular purpose is to give society a single day of respite from work.

As one might suppose, several pressure groups push these antiaid arguments. Americans United for Separation of Church and State is one of them, claiming over 200,000 members. It publishes a rather vociferous monthly magazine, *Church-State Review*, that devotes much space to the educational aid issue. For many years the National Council of Churches, speaking for the larger Protestant denominations, has been a vigorous opponent of state aid to parochial education, and the largest Protestant denomination not associated with the NCC, the Southern Baptists, is represented in Washington D.C. by the antiaid Baptist Joint Committee on Public Affairs. The American Jewish Congress has been active against aid as have two other Jewish groups—the American Jewish Committee and B'nai B'rith. The American Civil Liberties Union always takes a strict separationist position on such matters in both its national and state organizations. Not surprisingly, the National Education Association is generally opposed to support for private education.[15]

This discussion must leave the champion of liberty in a quandary. The two sides each bottom their case on freedom of religion. A person must choose sides and make an enemy in the choice or find a compromise position. Since some supporters of parochial aid want a great deal of aid, and since some opponents of it are still trying to overturn the Everson case that allowed payment for bus transportation to church-related schools, no compromise can satisfy all. The aim must be to create only the least offense.

Perhaps modest tax credits—that is, flat deductions from some tax bill—to parents of parochial school students would give least offense. They have these advantages: they are visible aid. If kept modest in amount, it could be argued that they help cover only the more secular costs of the schools. They are indirect, not involving the state with the schools' administration. They do not come out of the tax revenues that antiaid people help build up. Of course, they will be criticized by those who want more than modest aid and strongly attacked as unconstitutional by those who object to even indirect aids to church schools. Worst of all, the Supreme Court has already ruled them out. Thus, the hope for their acceptance rests on long-term education of the public-at-large, the shift of at least two judges to the accommodationist position, or on state and federal constitutional amendments. Years might be involved.

Prayer in Public Schools. After the Supreme Court wrote opinions banning school-sponsored devotional exercises in the early 1960s, some people argued that freedom to pray and read the Bible had been ended in the schools. From the justices' point of view this argument rested on a flat misunderstanding of the decisions.

All the justices treated the prayer and Bible reading cases as litigation, raising only an issue under the establishment clause—not under the free exercise clause. In a nutshell, they held that governments were forbidden from carrying out religious activities by the former clause. That is, "state religion" violated the Constitution. In the opinions, no question was raised about any private person's freedom to pray or read the Bible.

Certainly, if a pupil at the start of the school day or of a class period chooses to pray silently in nondisruptive ways, that pupil has done nothing the Court even considered in its prayer decisions. And it may be assumed with much confidence that if at recess, lunch hour, or other free time, a group of students on their own initiative chooses to pray or read Scripture together in ways that do not disrupt others' activities or that do not make a captive audience of their peers, such action is not forbidden by the prayer decisions.

Of course, if someone's prayer interrupts school activities, if it takes the student away from regularly scheduled programs, or if it is forced upon others due to their attendance at school, the school may disallow the prayer. Disruption of the classroom has never been a right of free expression.[16] In this respect the classroom and the pupil are like the government office and the government employee. No one argues that an employee may take time out of her eight-hour day for devotionals. Nor would anyone argue that a soldier may leave his battle station for prayers. At law, to everything there is a season and a time to every purpose under heaven.

Obviously also, if a school allowed a student to say "private devotionals" over the school intercom or at the start of an assembly, the courts would say that this private exercise was really a school supported, public devotional. And in all probability, courts will treat a school's student government as if it were a part of the school's administrative structure.

What is banned is devotional exercises that are organized and/or promoted by school officials or by people acting with school assistance or under color of school authority.

Is a teacher on his own initiative free to pray or read the Bible in a devotional or worshipful way in the school? The Court did not speak directly to this, but we can assume some answers. If it is silently done in free time—that is, in time for which the teacher is not paid—then the teacher would not violate the constitutional limit. But a qualification is in order. If the teacher did this when the pupils were present— just before class began, for example—in a manner that might influence them, the Court's limits would almost certainly apply. The teacher is a state employee, an authority figure. State school attendance laws cannot be used to round up an audience for the teacher's religious witness. Thus, the time period in which the teacher did this would not alone decide its legality. Influence would be another issue.

All this says that the Supreme Court did not limit the freedom of religion of pupils or teachers in its prayer decisions, *unless pupils and teachers claim it is their right to have devotionals wherever and whenever they please regardless of effects on others and on other activity or unless those people claim it is their right to participate in governmentally sponsored prayers.*

As far as I can find, few, if any, people make the first of these claims. If either claim is made, it runs head-on into the limits of the establishment clause. That clause decrees that governments have no religious functions, and it has been interpreted broadly enough to mean that governments cannot use their authority to promote religion.

At least one court of appeals decision decided a case concerning prayers in the classroom where the free exercise claim was central.[17] Some parents in Whitestone, New York, tried to enjoin school officials from forbidding joint recitation of "milk and cookie" prayers *in the classroom during school time with teachers in supervision.* Skeptical of the claim that the prayer was not school led, Judge Friendly, nevertheless, wrote the opinion assuming the prayer was truly spontaneous. Yet, he held that it was no violation of freedom of religion for New York to limit such group devotionals to protect itself from the charge of establishing religion. Freedom of religion is not, he said, freedom of groups to pray in state owned facilities "wherever and whenever they desire." To him, a "student's compelled presence in school five days a week in no way renders the regular religious facilities of the community less accessible to him than they are to others." He qualified the opinion for such possible exceptions as Moslems whose religion obliges them to bow to Mecca at specific times or for a child who could not eat cookies and milk without prayer. Such pupils, he said, might make a claim to be excused from class for a brief time for their private praying.

This discussion raises an important issue related to religion and the state not touched on before in this book. Some peoples' religion may be called *civil religion.* To them religious belief and expression are tightly tied, consciously or unconsciously, to the nation-state. Some of these regard their nation as God's chosen people, and they think of their nation's actions as an important part of God's expression of himself in history. This civil religion, say some scholars, is a separate religion in our society as well as in other societies. It stands alongside of, and importantly independent of, traditional Catholic, Protestant, and Jewish religions, though it may borrow from these.Indeed, it is a competitor with these religions in important respects.[18]

For at least some folk who hold to this civil religion, governmentally organized prayer may be a religious necessity. They may find their lives empty unless the nation-state acts as a sort of priest on their behalf, aiding their approach to God. From this perspective, the Supreme Court's decisions on prayer did deny freedom of religion.

Clearly, such a perspective makes the American scheme of church-state relations improper at its very foundations. There can be no separation of church and state as it has been authoritatively interpreted in most of our history, if civil religion is to prevail. In that religion, church and state are inextricably intertwined.

Whatever the impact and reality of civil religion, many Americans want prayer in the public schools—even in schools where prayers had not been said due to state and local rules for decades before the Supreme Court wrote its opinions on the subject. The Survey Research Center at the University of Michigan asked a large sample of Americans if they favored prayer in public schools in 1964 and again in 1968. Here are the results.

Prayer in Public Schools (Percentages) [19]

	1964	1968
Favor	74.9	73.4
Oppose	15.0	13.2
No Opinion	(n = 1566)	(n = 1327)

These percentages show that the Supreme Court's prayer decisions, however logical in terms of the long-standing meaning of the establishment clause, are not accepted or understood by Americans. The claims that the Court "banned prayer" or "threw God out of the schools," while wrong, are probably believed by many. Yet efforts at prayer amendments have failed, though such amendments are proposed in each session of the Congress.[20]

Obviously, here the First Amendment as used by nine judges overrides majority desires. Is this undemocratic? Yes. However, the Bill of Rights was adopted to thwart a large majority as well as a small minority. Majority rule and an effective Bill of Rights always stand in a potentially hostile relationship. Unless this is understood, the American Constitution is not understood.

Is there any way to satisfy those who want prayers in schools and still support the Supreme Court's interpretation of the establishment clause? Yes. At least some people could readily accept this suggestion. The purely private prayers of individual pupils or voluntary group prayers and Bible reading on free time were not restricted by the Court's opinion. The students who want such devotionals can have them if they will accept these limitations: the practices cannot disrupt school schedules in any way; they cannot interfere with other student activities in any way; they cannot be so located or scheduled that they would have a captive audience of nonparticipating students; and they cannot be organized or advertised or otherwise promoted by school authorities, including student government leaders. If individual students or voluntary groups would follow the spirit of these limitations, they would not be restricted by either school authority or by courts in all probability. If they were restricted, they would have an excellent chance of defending themselves in a court case.

Further and more important, if these suggestions were followed, the devotionals would be far more meaningful to most participants than devotionals initiated by school authorities.

Freedom and Responsibility

In this land there is a vast realm of religious freedom. There is also a far smaller realm of unfreedom. The existence of both realms ensures that contested territory claims attention.

Since liberty cannot be absolute, a free land will never lack for disputes. The question for our nation is not whether these disputes arise. Rather, it is our disposition in handling them. Does our posture bend toward freedom? Do we seek to settle disputes by maximizing liberty as much as prudently possible? Do we educate ourselves to accept an expression of belief tomorrow we were not able to accept today? Are we an open society?

If our nation can answer these questions positively, well and good. Yet such answers are just the starting point for the Christian. Having freedom, a further question is asked of us. How do we use it? Do we use it to promote the good life by our standards? *Liberty is for something. It is not an end in itself.* It is for the most ideal society and people we can develop in its realm. It is a means to a higher end.

A person in a slave state might be excused for not expressing his or her deepest insights. Not us. With our abundant freedom, we have a responsibility to use it for the common good. Paradoxically, liberty gives more, not less, duty.

Notes

1 Richard Bauman, "Snake Handling: Should It Be Banned?" *Liberty*, Vol. 70, No. 3, May–June, 1975, pp. 2–5.

[2] For a brief historic summary of conscientious objection in the United States, see Anson Phelps Stokes and Leo Pfeffer, *Church and State in the United States,* rev. ed. (New York: Harper and Row, 1964), pp. 474–478. Other relevant works include: Arlo Tatum, ed., *Handbook for Conscientious Objectors,* 11th ed. (Philadelphia: CCCO, An Agency for Military and Draft Counseling, 1970); Lillian Schissel, ed., *Conscience in America* (New York: E. P. Dutton and Co., 1968; James Finn, ed., *A Conflict of Loyalties* (New York: Pegasus, 1968); Sol Tax, ed., *The Draft* (Chicago: Chicago University Press, 1967).

[3] See a discussion of draft law development in the last thirty years in Raymond Wilson, *Uphill for Peace: Quaker Impact on Congress* (Richmond, Indiana: Friends United Press, 1975), pp. 189–213.

[4] For good chapter-long summaries of the law on this, see Richard E. Morgan, *The Supreme Court and Religion* (New York: The Free Press, 1972) and Leo Pfeffer, *God, Caesar and the Constitution* (Boston: Beacon Press, 1975).

[5] For a book that takes up the connection between religious liberty and conscience, see Milton R. Konvitz, *Religious Liberty and Conscience* (New York: The Viking Press, 1968).

[6] United States v. Sisson, 297 F. Supp. 902 (D. Mass. 1969).

[7] A continuing source for all these arguments in the magazine, *Freedom in Education* published by Citizens for Educational Freedom. For two often-cited, non-Catholic articles on this theme, see Will Herberg, "The Sectarian Conflict over Church and State," *Commentary* 14:5 November, 1952, pp. 450–462 and Wilbur G. Katz, "The Freedom to Believe," *Atlantic Monthly* 192:4 October, 1953, pp. 66–69. For a compact argument by a Catholic, see Robert F. Drinan, "The Constitutionality of Public Aid to Parochial Schools," Dallin H. Oaks, ed., *The Wall Between Church and State* (Chicago: Phoenix Books, 1963). A prolific polemicist for this cause is Virgil C. Blum. See his *Freedom of Choice in Education* (New York: Macmillan, 1958) and *Freedom in Education* (New York: Doubleday, 1965). These writings, of course, are not all limited to the legal aspects of the matter as is the one made here.

[8] Abington School District v. Schempp, 374 U.S. 203 (1963).

[9] Virgil C. Blum, "The Supreme Court and Religion," *Vital Speeches* 40:11 March 15, 1974, pp. 337–338.

[10] Wilbur G. Katz, "The Freedom to Believe," *Atlantic Monthly* 192:4 October, 1953, pp. 66–69.

[11] Will Herberg, "The Sectarian Conflict over Church and State" and Milton Himmelfarb, "Church and State: How High a Wall?" *Commentary* 42:1 July, 1966, pp. 23–29.

[12] For a description of these groups, see Richard E. Morgan, *The Politics of Religious Conflict* (New York: Pegasus, 1968), pp. 60–68.

[13] For a magazine that devotes much space to this matter on a continuing basis, see *Church-State Review,* published by Americans United for Separation of Church and State. Other sources include Murray A. Gordon, "The Unconstitutionality of Public Aid to Parochial Schools," Dallin H. Oaks, ed., *The Wall*

Between Church and State (Chicago: Phoenix Books, 1963); George R. LaNoue, *Public Funds for Parochial Schools?* (New York: Department of Religious Liberty of the National Council of the Churches of Christ in the U.S.A., 1963); Joseph M. Dawson, *America's Way in Church, State and Society* (New York: Macmillan, 1953); Pfeffer, *God, Caesar and the Constitution.*

[14] Everson v. Board of Education, 330 U.S. 1 (1947).

[15] Morgan, *The Politics of Religious Conflict,* pp. 49–60.

[16] This was a part of the issue in Tinker v. Des Moines, 383 U.S. 503 (1969).

[17] Stein v. Oshinsky, 384 F. 2d 999 (1965).

[18] For writing on this subject, see Robert N. Bellah, "Civil Religion in America," *Daedalus,* Vol. 96, No. 1, Winter, 1967; Elwyn A. Smith, ed., *The Religion of the Republic* (Philadelphia: Fortress Press, 1971); Conrad Cherry, ed., *God's New Israel: Religious Interpretations of American Destiny* (Englewood Cliffs, New Jersey: Prentice Hall, 1971). For recent articles on this subject, see Robert D. Linder, "Civil Liberty in Historical Perspective: The Reality that Underlies the Concept" and Henry Warner Bowden, "A Historian's Response to the Concept of American Civil Religion," both in *Journal of Church and State,* Vol. 17, No. 3, Autumn, 1975, pp. 399–422 and 495–505.

[19] William C. Adams, "American Public Opinion in the 1960s on Two Church-State Issues," *Journal of Church and State,* Vol. 17, No. 3, Autumn, 1975, p. 479.

[20] Pfeffer, *God, Caesar and the Constitution,* pp. 213–220.

Index

183

TEXAS A&M UNIVERSITY LIBRARY